Career Planning for Teens

A Comprehensive Guide to Career Planning

(A Comprehensive Guide for Teens on Planning and Achieving Their Career Goals)

Carter Wilcox

Published By **Hailey Leigh**

Carter Wilcox

All Rights Reserved

Career Planning for Teens: A Comprehensive Guide to Career Planning (A Comprehensive Guide for Teens on Planning and Achieving Their Career Goals)

ISBN 978-0-9949563-7-8

No part of this guidebook shall be reproduced in any form without permission in writing from the publisher except in the case of brief quotations embodied in critical articles or reviews.

Legal & Disclaimer

The information contained in this book is not designed to replace or take the place of any form of medicine or professional medical advice. The information in this book has been provided for educational & entertainment purposes only.

The information contained in this book has been compiled from sources deemed reliable, and it is accurate to the best of the Author's knowledge; however, the Author cannot guarantee its accuracy and validity and cannot be held liable for any errors or omissions. Changes are periodically made to this book. You must consult your doctor or get professional medical advice before using any of the suggested remedies, techniques, or information in this book.

Upon using the information contained in this book, you agree to hold harmless the Author from and against any damages, costs, and expenses, including any legal fees potentially resulting from the application of any of the information provided by this guide. This disclaimer applies to any damages or injury caused by the use and application, whether directly or indirectly, of any advice or information presented, whether for breach of contract, tort, negligence, personal injury, criminal intent, or under any other cause of action.

You agree to accept all risks of using the information presented inside this book. You need to consult a professional medical practitioner in order to ensure you are both able and healthy enough to participate in this program.

Table Of Contents

Chapter 1: Identifying Personal Strengths Weaknesses Values 1

Chapter 2: Researching Careers 11

Chapter 3: Setting Goals 24

Chapter 4: Building Your Resume 33

Chapter 5: Strategic Networking 44

Chapter 6: Mastering Interview Skills 64

Chapter 7: Entrepreneurship 79

Chapter 8: Continuing Education And Professional Development 87

Chapter 9: Coping With Setbacks and Challenges 99

Chapter 10: What Is An Apprenticeship? 112

Chapter 11: Understanding Yourself 166

Chapter 12: Smart Goals for Success 174

Chapter 13: Creating an Action Plan 180

Chapter 1: Identifying Personal Strengths Weaknesses Values

Welcome to the number one economic catastrophe of our complete manual, Career Planning Guide for Young Adults. As the decision shows, we can accompany you on a step-by way of using-step adventure toward finding your purpose, building your resume, and launching your profession. But earlier than diving into the realistic factors of career improvement, its miles essential to apprehend you better. After all, how will you select out a fulfilling career without spotting your particular combination of strengths, weaknesses, values, and hobbies? In this starting financial disaster, we are able to stroll you via a series of self-exploration sports activities designed to shed moderate on the ones crucial additives of your man or woman.

Identifying Personal Strengths

Strengths seek advice from the herbal capabilities, abilities, and dispositions that allow us to excel in top notch areas. When honed and done strategically, those assets can make contributions drastically to our fulfillment and happiness in each non-public and professional sphere. Unfortunately, many human beings neglect their innate items or fail to leverage them optimally. Therefore, taking inventory of your strengths early in your career planning technique is essential.

Begin through asking pals, own family participants, colleagues, or instructors to give an explanation for your superb traits and competencies. You can be amazed on the wealth of insights accumulated from out of doors perspectives. Next, list your accomplishments in the course of numerous domains—teachers, sports activities sports activities, arts, volunteer artwork, or precise extracurricular sports. Reflect on what enabled you to reach each instance. Were you in particular prepared? Creative? Persistent? Analytical? These traits probably represent a number of your center strengths.

Additionally, keep in mind the usage of online assessment equipment which incorporates StrengthsFinder, VIA Character Survey, or Marcus Buckingham's StandOut. These proof-based gadgets can offer valuable insights into your dominant abilities and corresponding career alternatives. Remember, but, that no unmarried take a look at can seize the general spectrum of human complexity. Thus, method the ones resources with an open mind and regard them as complementary in preference to definitive resources of self-expertise.

Recognizing Personal Weaknesses

While focusing on our strengths is important for reinforcing self notion and overall performance, neglecting areas requiring development can prevent improvement and restriction potential. Being aware about your weaknesses lets in you to are searching for centered assist, lessen blind spots, and keep humility—all important elements for prolonged-time period success.

Start by using manner of manner of acknowledging activities or conditions that drain your strength or bring about repeated struggles. Perhaps you grapple with public speaking, coping with price variety, or meeting deadlines. Once identified, decide whether or not or now not or not those weaknesses stem from a loss of talent, knowledge, or interest. If viable, make investments effort and time into strengthening these areas via exercise, take a look at, or schooling. Alternatively, keep in mind delegating obligations that rely closely on your susceptible elements to relied on collaborators whose strengths catch up to your deficiencies.

Values

Personal values encompass deeply held ideals regarding what's crucial, applicable, or profitable. They characteristic guiding standards that dictate our alternatives, behaviors, and priorities. Integrating values into career making plans ensures alignment amongst expert endeavors and personal convictions, therefore promoting success and technique pride.

To unearth your middle values, contemplate situations in which you felt proud, fulfilled, or inspired. Common values embody authenticity, compassion, excellence, fairness, freedom, honesty, integrity, loyalty, love, recognize, duty, safety, balance, spirituality, and keep in mind. Rank order those values steady with their relevance and non-negotiable reputation. Finally, evaluate how closely current-day or expected careers align along with your pinnacle-ranked values. Seek possibilities that resonate profoundly along with your notion tool to maximise which means that and leisure for your paintings lifestyles.

Interests

Simply located, pursuits speak over with sports or subjects that captivate and stimulate us. By exploring and prioritizing our interests, we growth the opportunities of selecting careers that hold engagement, assignment intellectual hobby, and spark intrinsic motivation.

Make a listing of pastimes, disciplines, or phenomena that ignite your hobby and excite your senses. Classify those gadgets into commands along facet modern, clinical, technical, social, bodily, or interpersonal. Then, probe deeper via carrying out mini-experiments, volunteering, activity shadowing, or internships to gauge compatibility with respective fields. Lastly, bypass-reference your findings in opposition to to be had career alternatives to slender down possible alternatives that promise sustained delight and gratification.

By making an investment time and effort into information ourselves higher, we lay the foundation for clever profession options rooted in self-cognizance, authenticity, and intentionality. With this sturdy base set up, next chapters will manual you via the final ranges of career making plans, culminating in a blueprint for achievement uniquely tailored for your awesome profile so buckle up, steeply-priced reader, as we hold this exhilarating adventure collectively.

Exploring Different Personality Types and how they relate to Careers

Personality Types and Career Selection

Your man or woman kind performs a great characteristic in identifying which career path suits you awesome. Various theories exist to categorize character patterns, however one notably general model is the Myers-Briggs Type Indicator (MBTI), which classifies individuals into 16 distinct businesses based mostly on four dichotomies: Extraversion vs Introversion, Sensing vs Intuition, Thinking vs Feeling, and Judging vs Perceiving. Let's look at how these dimensions have an effect on career choice.

Extraversion (E) vs Introversion (I)

Individuals who score excessive on extraversion generally tend to draw energy from interacting with others and running in team settings. Meanwhile, introverts determine upon quiet environments and derive pride from solo duties. Neither trait is advanced to the alternative; as an alternative, understanding in that you fall along this continuum permit you to pick out careers that cater to your selected mode of operation.

Sales representatives, occasion planners, marketers, politicians, and educators usually lean towards extroversion due to their want for normal interaction. On the opposite, writers, researchers, software software program developers, artists, and analysts frequently display off introverted dispositions, favoring unbiased paintings over group dynamics.

Sensing (S) vs Intuition (N)

Sensing types focus on tangible statistics, facts, facts, and immediate surroundings, whilst intuitive types cognizance on patterns, necessities, mind, and future implications. Both sensing and intuitive personalities make a contribution in any other case to problem-solving approaches.

Engineers, clinical experts, cops, chefs, and creation employees typically show sensing tendencies due to the reality accuracy, precision, and reliability underpin their day by day bodily video games. Conversely, architects, inventors, entrepreneurs, professionals, and architects encompass intuitive traits, constantly brainstorming novel answers and looking forward to future trends.

Thinking (T) vs Feeling (F)

Thinkers prioritize accurate judgment, objectivity, consistency, and rational assessment while making alternatives. Feelers, conversely, vicinity more weight on emotions, empathy, harmony, and interpersonal members of the own family. Although neither style surpasses the alternative in absolute terms, matching your choice-making desire with the right profession can cause increased method satisfaction and productiveness.

Managers, felony experts, scientists, engineers, and mathematicians frequently consist of questioning attitudes, valuing analytical rigor and impersonal judgement calls. Contrarily, counselors, therapists, social personnel, nurses, and teachers normally adopt feeling inclinations, centering care, warm temperature, and sensitivity of their line of obligation.

Judging (J) vs Perceiving (P)

Judgers respect set up schedules, predictability, closure, and decisiveness. Perceivers crave flexibility, spontaneity, adaptability, and open-endedness. Striking a balance some of the ones contrasting orientations remains crucial at the same time as taking into account careers.

Chapter 2: Researching Careers

Welcome to the second economic wreck of our whole manual, "Career Planning one 0 one for Young Adults." Having committed large attempt to facts yourself within the previous pages, you presently own a stronger draw near of your private strengths, weaknesses, values, pursuits, and person traits. This self-consciousness lays a crucial foundation for the subsequent phase of career exploration: reading capability careers that align together along with your particular identity.

Why commit lots time to investigating careers? Simply placed, arming yourself with accurate facts about severa professions lets in you to make informed alternatives concerning your future. Without sufficient studies, you chance getting into a region unsuited in your abilties, values, or personality, probably resulting in dissatisfaction, burnout, or wasted belongings.

In this bankruptcy, we are capable of demystify the profession research technique, revealing sensible strategies for amassing intel on industries, occupations, salaries, instructional requirements, and increase opportunities. Our purpose is twofold: first, to empower you with the gear important to behavior impartial explorations; and second, to instill behavior conducive to lifelong reading and flexibility in a unexpectedly changing global.

We will provoke our communicate through defining key terminology germane to career research, decided through an define of dependable property available at your fingertips. Subsequently, we are capable of outline a scientific method for distilling large portions of records into actionable insights, culminating in a custom designed profession roadmap. Along the way, we are capable of incorporate actual-international examples to demonstrate summary necessities, fostering readability and idea.

Whether you're in reality starting to entertain thoughts of your expert future or fine-tuning modern-day plans, relaxation confident that this financial ruin includes treasured guidance right to every diploma of career improvement. Together, we are able to traverse the labyrinthine realm of profession options, losing mild on promising paths nicely really worth of pursuit. Are you prepared to dive in? Let's start.

Discovering Potential Careers Through Online Resources, Informational Interviews, and Job Shadowing

Discovering Potential Careers

Before embarking on a deep dive into particular careers, it's crucial to strong a big internet and find out various alternatives. Three primary techniques for doing so embody on line research, informational interviews, and hobby shadowing. Let's take a look at out every technique in turn.

Online Resources

With infinite net web sites committed to profession exploration, it is an awful lot less tough than ever to collect preliminary records from the consolation of your home. Reputable databases collectively with O*NET, Bureau of Labor Statistics (BLS), and Department of Labor offer top notch profiles on loads of occupations, detailing commonplace obligations, median wages, educational necessities, projected increase costs, and nearby name for.

When perusing these web sites, pay close to interest to key terms that resonate collectively together with your pastimes, values, and competencies. Jot down notes on any career that piques your interest, noting professionals, cons, and lingering questions. Don't forget about to analyze adjacent roles within the equal organization, as those can also yield unexpected gem stones off the crushed route.

Informational Interviews

Supplementing digital research with actual-worldwide conversations offers depth and nuance to your facts of functionality careers. Enterprising individuals can request informational interviews with experts currently hired in fields of interest. Not nice do such dialogues offer firsthand debts of every day operations, however similarly they offer possibilities to ask pointed questions and glean insider insights unavailable some exclusive location.

To installation an informational interview, begin with the aid of accomplishing out on your extended network—pals, circle of relatives individuals, acquaintances, university alumni, or social media connections—to emerge as aware of potential contacts. Formulate a concise pitch explaining your intentions and with politeness requesting 20-1/2 of-hour in their time. Come prepared with a list of thoughtful queries showcasing your real interest and preference to take a look at. And endure in mind to ship a thank-you phrase in a while!

Job Shadowing

If possible, examine specialists performing their duties stay and in man or woman. Job shadowing offers brilliant get right of entry to to the inner workings of a given career, allowing you to witness the triumphs and tribulations professional by means of the use of practitioners each day. Plus, spending time immersed in a particular surroundings can validate (or contradict!) assumptions shaped finally of initial levels of discovery.

To arrange a interest shadowing enjoy, repeat the aforementioned steps for arranging informational interviews. Express your willingness to go to worksites, watch court docket docket cases spread, and assist with minor obligations. Ensure you dress accurately, arrive punctually, and preserve a courteous demeanor subsequently of the observation period. Should the possibility upward push up, capture it—activity shadowing may additionally moreover moreover verify (or dispel) misconceptions, gasoline motivation, and catalyze momentum within the route of your dream career.

In final, combining on-line sleuthing, face-to-face chats, and onsite observations paints a glittery portrait of capacity careers. By incorporating multiple viewpoints and mediums, you will amass a wealth of know-how priming you for the subsequent segment: significantly comparing located options vis-à-vis your non-public strengths, weaknesses, values, and pursuits.

Evaluating The Education, Training, and Experience Required for Various Careers

Now that you have located capability careers through on-line research, informational interviews, and mission shadowing, it's time to assess the education, training, and enjoy required for those fields. Gathering this data will assist you decide if a specific career aligns along side your modern-day state of affairs and destiny desires.

Education Requirements

Some careers mandate unique levels or levels of education, while others offer extra flexible get right of entry to routes. Familiarize yourself with the minimum academic requirements for each career on your list. Consult authoritative resources collectively with professional association net websites, authorities exertions information, and university branch pages. Make phrase of diploma names, concentrations, and credit score rating hours encouraged for achievement in your preferred field. Also, hold in thoughts whether or not or not on line, hybrid, or traditional lecture room formats higher in form your analyzing style and time desk constraints.

Training Programs

Often, professions name for supplementary training past formal schooling. Apprenticeships, certification courses, licensure tests, and persevering with education credit hold practitioners abreast of enterprise standards, technological enhancements, and moral pointers. Browse exchange guides, enterprise newsfeeds, and convention proceedings to stay up to date on emergent developments. Speak proper away with experts in your preferred vicinity to find out approximately lesser-recognized training opportunities that confer aggressive benefit.

Experience Matters

Real-global publicity distinguishes beginner candidates from seasoned veterans. Many employers privilege applicants who have finished internships, externships, summer time jobs, or volunteer art work associated with their favored profession. Accruing such stories signals willpower, initiative, and transferable skill development. Devise a way for garnering pertinent reviews both organically (e.G., part-time employment finally of excessive school or college) or deliberately (e.G., cold emailing corporations to request shadowing or informational interview opportunities.)

Relevant Experience Checklist:

- Internships/Externships
- Part-time Jobs
- Summer Employment
- Freelance Work
- Contract Projects
- Volunteer Opportunities
- Independent Study
- Capstone Projects
- Student Organizations
- Clubs & Societies
- Competitions
- Hackathons
- Case Studies
- Simulation Exercises
- Role Play Scenarios

Evaluate the relative importance of training, education, and experience for every career in your listing. Some fields can also emphasize formal training, at the equal time as others prioritize hands-on experience or specialized certifications. Balance your aspirations in opposition to practical concerns which includes cost, availability, and timelines. Realistically verify your functionality to obtain essential credentials and weigh the funding in competition to expected returns.

Summing Up

Discerning the training, schooling, and revel in required for numerous careers arms you with vital data for knowledgeable choice-making. Deliberately accumulating this information streamlines your search, saving precious time and assets. Articulating particular wishes simplifies verbal exchange with mentors, advisors, and recruiters, facilitating smoother transitions into your desired career.

Considering Salary Ranges, Work-Life Balance, and Future Growth Opportunities

Salary Ranges

One vital detail to take into account whilst studying careers is the potential income you can earn. Understanding average salaries for severa professions will allow you to make knowledgeable alternatives about which careers align collectively in conjunction with your economic desires and expectancies. It is crucial to appearance past the raw numbers and dig deeper into the repayment packages supplied via particular industries. Benefits inclusive of medical medical insurance, retirement contributions, bonuses, and paid break day can substantially impact your regularly occurring income and first-class of existence.

Start thru consulting dependable property like Glassdoor, Payscale, and the Bureau of Labor Statistics (BLS) to discover accurate earnings records to your selected profession. Be certain to clear out consequences primarily based on elements such as place, company length, and years of enjoy to get a extra correct estimate of what you'll likely earn in a selected feature. Remember that salaries can variety extensively depending on these variables, so it's far vital to have a realistic records of what to expect.

Work-Life Balance

Another vital interest while coming across careers is paintings-existence balance. The time period refers back to the equilibrium amongst an man or woman's professional and private lives. Achieving a healthful artwork-existence balance manner having true sufficient time and energy for each career obligations and personal pursuits, interests, and relationships. Poor paintings-lifestyles balance can motive burnout, reduced productiveness, and diminished ordinary nicely-being.

Chapter 3: Setting Goals

Congratulations! You've taken significant strides in expertise yourself and getting to know functionality careers that align together collectively along with your pastimes, values, and skills. Now it is time to channel that know-how into actionable steps in the path of reaching your career aspirations. That's in which aim setting is to be had in.

Goal putting is a virtually effective tool for turning indistinct goals into tangible reality. It offers a roadmap for your career adventure, retaining you centered, stimulated, and committed to your selected direction. Effective cause putting consists of more than casually wishing for success; it requires cautious concept, planned making plans, and ordinary effort.

In this financial ruin, we will discover diverse factors of purpose placing, from figuring out precise, measurable, practicable, applicable, and time-high-quality (SMART) wants to developing strategies for monitoring development and overcoming barriers. We'll moreover communicate the significance of aligning your goals at the side of your values and imaginative and prescient to your destiny, as well as the area of motivation and responsibility in the usage of long-term success.

First, we are going to define key terms and ideas related to purpose setting, drawing on highbrow research and real-worldwide examples to illustrate their importance. Next, we are going to delve into the machine of setting SMART desires, walking you thru each aspect and providing realistic guidelines for utilizing this framework for your very own career aspirations.

After installing your SMART goals, we're going to shift our interest to designing movement plans that convert your goals into achievable steps. We'll explore numerous strategies for breaking down complex duties, prioritizing competing desires, and allocating assets effectively. Throughout this speak, we are capable of emphasize the charge of pliability and versatility in responding to inevitable setbacks and worrying conditions.

Of path, aim setting isn't certainly about mechanics and method; it's also about tapping into your inner pressure and keeping momentum over the years. Accordingly, we're going to take a look at the position of motivation in fueling your pursuit of career achievement, regarding each intrinsic and extrinsic assets of motivation and discussing strategies for retaining engagement and exuberance even if faced with adversity.

Accountability is a few different crucial aspect of effective reason setting. Whether you enlist the guide of pals, family individuals, mentors, or coaches, having someone else maintain you responsible for your improvement can extensively decorate your possibilities of carrying out your desires. We'll find out severa obligation systems and advocate strategies for incorporating them into your purpose-placing tool.

Finally, we will wrap up this monetary damage by means of discussing the significance of celebrating milestones and acknowledging achievements along the way. Taking time to understand your development not best feels specific—it additionally reinforces amazing behaviors and strengthens your remedy to hold striving for success.

So, allow's roll up our sleeves and dive into the exciting international of reason placing! By studying the artwork of placing and attaining SMART dreams, you'll be well in your manner to remodeling your career aspirations into reality.

Defining Short-Term and Long-Term Career Goals

Now that you have a sturdy information of the significance of putting profession desires, it's time to delve into the specifics of defining your brief-time period and lengthy-term dreams. Distinguishing between the ones kinds of goals will help you create a nicely-rounded and balanced profession plan that addresses each right away goals and destiny aspirations.

Short-Term Career Goals

Short-time period profession dreams are dreams that may be performed inner a significantly brief duration, typically beginning from numerous months to more than one years. These desires function stepping stones inside the path of your prolonged-time period imaginative and prescient, offering you with a enjoy of route and cause within the near term.

Some examples of quick-time period career goals encompass:

Acquiring a contemporary capability or certification

Securing a promoting or growth

Expanding your expert community

Changing jobs or industries

Starting a side hustle or small industrial agency

When defining your short-time period career desires, take into account the following recommendations:

Specific: Clearly define what you desire to achieve, the use of actionable language and urban metrics.

Example: "Improve my public talking skills by means of manner of turning in 5 indicates at neighborhood organisation sports within the subsequent year."

Measurable: Establish requirements for gauging your development and achievement.

Example: "Complete a six-week public speaking route and get maintain of first-class remarks from as a minimum 3 target audience participants at every occasion."

Achievable: Ensure your desires are practical, given your contemporary-day capabilities diploma, belongings, and opportunities.

Example: "Research neighborhood enterprise business enterprise sports and understand 5 suitable venues for giving presentations."

Relevant: Confirm that your goals align collectively along with your lengthy-term vision and broader profession objectives.

Example: "Public talking abilities will decorate my credibility and visibility interior my business enterprise, making me a greater attractive candidate for promotions and management roles."

Time-positive: Specify a cut-off date for completing each reason, growing a sense of urgency and galvanizing centered attempt.

Example: "Deliver the number one presentation interior six months of beginning the overall public speakme course."

Long-Term Career Goals

Long-time period profession dreams are goals that require huge time, try, and dedication to realise, regularly extending beyond 5 years into the destiny. These goals encapsulate your closing profession aspirations and provide an overarching framework for structuring your expert development efforts.

Some examples of lengthy-term profession goals encompass:

Achieving a senior-diploma function interior your present day organisation

Transitioning into a totally new vicinity or corporation

Earning a graduate diploma or expert designation

Starting your very non-public business or becoming a diagnosed authority on your place

Making a full-size impact to your network or agency through advocacy, innovation, or philanthropy

When defining your prolonged-term profession desires, adhere to the following ideas:

Visionary: Imagine an inspiring and ambitious future state that motivates and energizes you.

Example: "Establish myself as a reputable chief in sustainable city development, spearheading current-day-day tasks that sell ecological preservation, social equity, and financial viability."

Comprehensive: Capture the breadth and depth of your career aspirations, accounting for various additives of professional boom and achievement.

Example: "Develop information in green infrastructure, transportation planning, and public insurance; construct a robust expert community of like-minded friends and mentors; and advocate for revolutionary pointers that foster sustainable groups."

Flexible: Remain open to changes and recalibrations as you have a observe, expand, and adapt to converting situations.

Chapter 4: Building Your Resume

A Crucial Component of Career Success

As you embark to your profession journey, one essential tool to your arsenal is a properly-crafted resume. Serving as your expert calling card, your resume introduces you to functionality employers, conveys your qualifications, and differentiates you from exceptional candidates. Indeed, your resume acts as a gatekeeper, figuring out whether or not you proceed to the following round of the hiring system or land inside the rejected pile.

But what precisely constitutes a stellar resume? How are you able to effectively communicate your strengths, achievements, and capacity charge to functionality employers? And how do you tailor your resume to precise hobby openings, ensuring maximum enchantment and relevance?

These questions and extra lie on the coronary coronary heart of this economic catastrophe, which tackles the artwork and technological understanding of building an exquisite, impactful resume. From expertise the critical components of a winning resume to customizing your file for numerous roles and industries, we're going to discover attempted-and-right techniques for elevating your resume undertaking and catching the eye of hiring managers.

Along the way, we are going to debunk not unusual myths and misconceptions about resume-building, converting antique advice with present day excellent practices informed through the state-of-the-art research and employer expectancies. We'll moreover delve into the nuances of resume format, format, and length, assisting you strike the touchy balance between aesthetics and substance.

Armed with this information, you'll be well-prepared to create a resume that certainly presentations your specific mixture of talents, studies, and aspirations – a resume that now not simplest receives decided but additionally propels you in advance in your profession adventure.

Highlighting Relevant Experiences, Achievements, and Skills: Showcasing Your Best Self

Among the most crucial elements of crafting a standout resume is efficiently highlighting your applicable reviews, achievements, and capabilities. This section of our profession planning guide for young adults delves into the nuts and bolts of talking your qualifications in a way that appeals to capability employers and gadgets you other than the opposition.

Identifying Relevant Experiences

Not all reviews are created equal almost about impressing capacity employers. Your project is to sift via your information and pinpoint the ones stories that align maximum cautiously with the assignment posting's necessities and the employer's mission and values.

Begin via the use of growing a entire listing of your previous roles, internships, volunteer positions, and extracurricular sports activities. Then, carefully assessment the system description, paying precise interest to the listed qualifications, duties, and preferred abilties. Cross-reference this facts collectively together with your research, looking for overlap and synergies.

For instance, assume you are applying for a advertising coordinator role at a tech startup. Among your testimonies, you will likely highlight a summer time spent interning at a virtual enterprise, in that you controlled customer campaigns, achieved marketplace studies, and analyzed campaign overall performance. Or probably you served as president of your university's marketing membership, organizing speaker collection, networking sports, and branding responsibilities. Either manner, connecting the dots among your opinions and the mission requirements demonstrates your readiness for the feature.

Showcasing Quantifiable Achievements

Numbers speak, specially in relation to proving your clearly truely well worth to capacity employers. Whenever possible, decrease returned up your claims with concrete information, illustrating the tangible effect you have were given had on beyond responsibilities and businesses.

Continuing with our advertising and advertising and marketing and marketing coordinator example, don't forget you oversaw a scholar-led advertising and marketing and advertising campaign for a campus occasion, producing $5,000 in rate price tag earnings and attracting hundred attendees. Presenting the ones figures to your resume proper now conveys your effectiveness, credibility, and rate proposition. Similarly, bringing up that you grew a Twitter following through 25% or reduced soar fee on a internet internet site with the useful resource of using 10% speaks volumes approximately your capacity to pressure results.

However, now not all achievements lend themselves effects to numerical representation. Sometimes, qualitative accomplishments deliver same weight, signaling your ingenuity, adaptability, or leadership prowess. Think creatively approximately the testimonies you tell and the messages you bring, painting a colorful image of your contributions and successes.

Spotlighting Key Skills

Modern resumes frequently function a separate section devoted explicitly to list relevant abilities. This segment gives an outstanding opportunity to broadcast your talents, specially once they span severa roles, industries, or contexts.

Begin through drafting a complete inventory of your talents, dividing them into categories which include technical, interpersonal, and transferable. Then, pare down the listing, keeping pleasant those most relevant to the position on hand.

Technical capabilities embody specialised expertise or skillability specifically gadget, structures, or methodologies. Depending at the technique, those may additionally embody coding languages, photograph format software application, statistical evaluation techniques, or foreign places languages.

Interpersonal talents talk in your potential to paintings effectively with others, whether or no longer or no longer taking part with colleagues, negotiating with clients, or dealing with stakeholders. Communication, battle choice, empathy, and lively listening determine most of the maximum prized interpersonal abilties.

Transferable skills pass beyond character roles, industries, or contexts, representing common abilities that look at anyplace you bypass. Problem-fixing, critical questioning, adaptability, time control, and management exemplify such transferable capabilities.

Strategies for Effective Self-Promotion

To make certain your applicable reports, achievements, and talents shine thru on your resume, remember the subsequent techniques:

Use motion verbs and robust adjectives to frame your testimonies and accomplishments, demonstrating your initiative, effect, and consequences orientation.

Customize your resume for each method software, emphasizing those elements of your history that align maximum cautiously with the vicinity's requirements and the business employer's assignment.

Lead together along side your maximum brilliant achievements and qualifications, grabbing the reader's interest from the outset and compelling them to preserve studying.

Focus on the charge you introduced to beyond roles, framing your contributions in phrases of the troubles you solved, the efficiencies you gained, and the income you generated.

Provide context on your achievements, describing the scope and scale of your duties, the annoying situations you confronted, and the assets at your disposal.

Avoid hyperbolic statements or exaggerated claims, sticking as an opportunity to the information and letting your accomplishments talk for themselves.

By efficiently highlighting your relevant studies, achievements, and skills, you display your fitness for the location and signal your functionality to make a distinction in the enterprise company. With a nicely-crafted resume in hand, you're one step in the direction of touchdown your dream task and kickstarting your career.

Tailoring Resumes to Specific Jobs or Industries: Maximizing Impact and Appeal

In ultra-current fiercely aggressive project market, a ordinary, one-length-fits-all resume really might not lessen it. Employers accumulate dozens, if no longer masses, of packages for every emptiness, making it incumbent upon you to tailor your resume to the high-quality assignment or company in question.

Customizing your resume to each software program indicates capacity employers that you've finished your homework, recognize their wishes and values, and possess the competencies and critiques critical to hit the floor going for walks. By assessment, failing to tailor your resume runs the danger of acting lazy, disconnected, or ill-organized, jeopardizing your chances of touchdown an interview or securing the placement.

In this phase, we discover the artwork and technological understanding of tailoring your resume to specific jobs or industries, protecting the whole thing from key-word optimization and formatting tweaks to strategic omissions and additions.

Keyword Optimization: Demonstrating Affinity with Industry Lingo and Expectations

Keywords play a crucial position in getting your resume past computerized applicant tracking systems (ATS) and into the palms of human selection-makers. These software program software software gear take a look at digital submissions for specific terms and terms, sorting licensed applicants from the share.

To maximize your possibilities of passing muster with ATS algorithms, comb thru the way posting and extract applicable key phrases, incorporating them seamlessly into your resume. These can also additionally encompass industry buzzwords, technical terminology, or specific qualifications said inside the venture description.

Chapter 5: Strategic Networking

Networking – the apparently mystical paintings of forging connections, constructing relationships, and replacing favors – holds huge energy for young adults navigating the treacherous waters of profession planning. Often overlooked as manipulative, transactional, or opportunistic, networking although stands as a cornerstone of professional development, fueling profession increase, sparking collaborations, and starting off doorways to untapped opportunities.

In this phase, we demystify networking, casting apart awful stereotypes and unmasking its real ability as a automobile for personal and professional transformation. We explore the who, what, in which, while, why, and the way of networking, arming you with the facts, capabilities, and self belief to forge sizeable connections that catapult you closer to your desires.

Who Should I Network With?

Everyone and anybody. Cast a huge net, attractive with human beings from severa backgrounds, industries, and walks of lifestyles. Friends, own family individuals, former colleagues, professors, alumni, mentors, recruiters, and strangers all qualify as capability nodes in your ever-increasing network.

Approach networking with an widespread mentality, viewing every interplay as a threat to analyze, grow, and alternate charge. Eschew slim-mindedness or prejudice, embracing variety and inclusivity as guiding principles. Remember that serendipity regularly moves whilst least anticipated, so stay open to surprises and serendipitous encounters along the manner.

What Is Networking?

At its center, networking consists of forming collectively beneficial relationships characterised via accept as real with, reciprocity, and shared desires. Far from exploitative or self-serving, networking revolves round real communicate, lively listening, and genuine connection.

Effective networking needs vulnerability, humility, and hobby, developments seldom associated with shallow satisfied-handing or superficial banter. Approach networking as a conduit for non-public and expert increase, viewing each communique as an opportunity to increase your horizons, assignment your assumptions, and refine your worldview.

Where Can I Network?

Opportunities for networking abound, lurking in simple sight if best you dare to appearance. Traditional bastions of networking embody conferences, alternate shows, assignment fairs, mixers, and alumni sports, notwithstanding the reality that such gatherings rarely monopolize the scene.

Seek out unconventional venues for forging connections, collectively with museums, parks, cafés, gyms, libraries, or cultural gala's. Electronic dance song (EDM) festivals, comedian e-book conventions, or Dungeons & Dragons tournaments could in all likelihood seem now not going crucibles for expert bonding, but they harbor untapped functionality for kindred spirits in search of common ground.

When Should I Network?

Never save you networking. View courting-building as a lifelong company, continuously cultivating ties and fostering connections no matter your employment recognition, age, or station in existence.

Carpe diem, seizing fleeting moments to forge bonds with like-minded souls. Attend lectures, panels, or workshops, introducing your self to audio device, panelists, or fellow attendees. Strike up conversations with seatmates on airplanes, buses, or trains, probing under floor-diploma pleasantries to locate hidden depths and shared passions.

Why Should I Network?

Networking greases the wheels of fortune, lubricating your passage through existence's vicissitudes. Connections begat connections, multiplying exponentially as you ascend the ladder of achievement, putting in doorways to formerly unimagined realms of opportunity.

A strong community offers a ways extra than mere get right of entry to to undertaking opportunities or insider data. Robust relationships deliver moral guide, steerage, mentorship, friendship, and camaraderie, buffering you in opposition to adversity and bolstering your resilience within the face of challenges.

How Can I Network Effectively?

Authenticity trumps artifice. Be yourself, radiating warm temperature, generosity, and sincerity as you engage with others. Listen actively, posing thoughtful questions that betray your actual hobby and fascination.

Offer fee freely, sharing your records, insights, or property without expectation of reward. Practice the Platinum Rule, treating others as they want to be handled, touchy to their specific choices, customs, and idiosyncrasies.

Follow up diligently, sending nicely timed thank-you notes, articles, or hyperlinks that reference your conversations. Circulate amongst humans, playing the connector, brokering introductions, and facilitating partnerships.

In sum, networking ranks a number of the most terrific guns on your profession making plans arsenal, unlocking latent opportunities and laying waste to boundaries that when seemed insurmountable. Embrace the paintings of networking, harnessing its boundless functionality to enhance up your journey towards professional success and personal blossoming.

Building Relationships with Professionals in Your Desired Field

(Laying the Foundation for Long-Term Success)

Relationships shape the bedrock of any a success profession, serving as pillars of manual, guidance, and possibility. To thrive in your selected hassle, you have to cultivate sturdy connections with pro specialists who can illuminate the route beforehand, impart pearls of knowledge, and champion your cause at the same time as opportunities stand up.

Below, we define severa strategies for forging sizable relationships with experts in your desired domain, ensuring which you purchased the myriad advantages of mentorship, sponsorship, and alliance.

Identify Potential Mentors

Commence via manner of pinpointing people whose understanding, revel in, and achievements resonate on the facet of your aspirations and values. Peruse LinkedIn profiles, corporation guides, or expert establishments to gather a shortlist of luminaries surely properly well worth pursuing.

Cast your net huge, focused on professionals at various stages of seniority and specialties, widening your purview and exposing you to a kaleidoscope of views, insights, and warfare tales.

Initiate Contact

Broaching unknown territory can show intimidating, but worry and trepidation have to not deter you from attaining out to ability mentors. Initiate contact gracefully, showing reverence for his or her accomplishments while conveying your actual enthusiasm and admiration.

Compose a succinct, well mannered electronic mail, in short introducing yourself, outlining your dreams, and expressing your preference to investigate from their sage advise. Reference shared pursuits, reviews, or affiliations, fostering an instant connection and lowering protecting limitations.

Provide Value

Growing relationships necessitates reciprocity, a -manner avenue predicated on mutual advantage and shared fee. Before soliciting advice, useful resource, or endorsements, boom olive branches, proffering your offerings, knowledge, or sources in pass again.

Volunteer to assist with projects, activities, or reasons that align collectively along with your mentor's challenge, demonstrating your commitment, strength of mind, and observe-via. Contribute to on-line boards, communicate boards, or social media channels frequented by way of using your mentor, together with fee, sparking debate, and showcasing your thoughts and acumen.

Foster Authenticity

Transparency and candor underpin enduring relationships, built on accept as true with, empathy, and vulnerability. Be yourself, divulging your fears, foibles, and frailties, permitting your shield to drop and your proper essence to emerge.

Authenticity breeds intimacy, forging unbreakable bonds that withstand trials, tribulations, and tempests. Share your dreams, hopes, and aspirations, trying to find solace and sanctuary in the bosom of your mentor's knowledge and sagacity.

Express Gratitude

Thankfulness is going an prolonged way, manifesting itself in gestures grand and petite, verbal and written, public and personal. Never underestimate the electricity of a heartfelt "thank you," located through manner of the use of tokens of esteem, homage, or affection.

Send handwritten notes, present playing cards, or wonder bouquets, expressing your gratitude for the time, power, and attempt expended for your behalf. Publicly widely known your mentor's contributions, lauding their virtues, magnanimity, and largesse.

Persevere

Patience, perseverance, and staying energy distinguish champions from also-rans, retaining apart winners from losers. Relationships blossom through the years, requiring smooth loving care, moderate nurturance, and unwavering devotion.

Persisting via intervals of uncertainty, confusion, or estrangement assessments the mettle of even the maximum steadfast acolytes. Steel your self for occasional disappointments, dashed hopes, or damaged guarantees, soldiering onward until brighter skies seem on the horizon.

Attend Events and Conferences

Events and conferences convene corporation titans, perception leaders, and developing stars beneath one roof, imparting fertile ground for nascent connections to sprout and bloom. Arm your self with commercial organisation cards, an elevator pitch, and a grin, eagerly wearing out spirited conversations that veer off script, transcending small speak and platitudes.

Listen actively, absorbing information, insights, and anecdotes that beautify your knowledge and growth your horizons. Parlay danger encounters into lasting relationships, shopping for and selling touch information and scheduling check-up conferences to deepen your rapport.

Engage on Social Media Platforms

LinkedIn, Twitter, Instagram, and Facebook provide springboards for launching virtual interactions that morph into real-global relationships. Comment, like, and percentage posts that resonate collectively at the side of your pastimes, values, or dreams, frequently insinuating your self into the focus of your digital contemporaries.

Extol the virtues of idea leaders, amplifying their voices, and echoing their sentiments.

Curate content material that advances your narrative, burnishing your brand, and cementing your reputation as a valued contributor to the zeitgeist.

Join Professional Associations or Interest Groups

Associations and interest businesses teem with like-minded human beings united via shared passions, goals, or identities. Immerse your self in their midst, contributing to discussions, attending conferences, and volunteering for committees or jogging groups.

Should opportunities knock, answer the call, leveraging your newfound relationships to propel yourself in advance. Apply for awards, scholarships, or offers that apprehend incredible achievements or capability, cementing your stature as a developing celebrity.

Request Informational Interviews

Informational interviews offer structures for deciding on the brains of professional specialists, gleaning insights, and crystallizing your data of their adventure. Frame your requests humbly, expressing your admiration for his or her accomplishments and seeking out steering on navigating similar terrain.

Prepare diligently, crafting incisive questions that elicit massive solutions, probing the contours of their experience, and illuminating capacity pitfalls or shortcuts. Synthesize the facts gleaned, integrating it into your highbrow map, and calibrating your compass for that reason.

Cultivate Empathy and Active Listening

Empathy and energetic listening shape cornerstones of powerful relationships, fostering connections that run deeper than pores and skin deep. Suspend judgment, silencing your internal critic, and suspending disbelief as you immerse yourself within the worldview of your interlocutors.

Validate their feelings, reviews, or views, mirroring their body language, nodding assent, and voicing settlement. Paraphrase their statements, checking for facts, and retaining their contributions.

Follow Up

Follow-up emails, messages, or letters make more potent your commitment, signaling your seriousness and solve. Summarize key takeaways, reaffirming your appreciation for his or her time, power, and insights.

Circle lower decrease back periodically, updating your mentors on your development, looking for feedback, or soliciting advice. Foster a rhythm that fits each activities, carving out slots for entice-ups, coffees, or lunches that make more potent your bond.

In end, constructing relationships with specialists for your favored concern wishes courage, conviction, and resilience. By embracing these strategies, you can domesticate a community of supporters, publications, and champions who champion your purpose, cast off darkness out of your route, and propel you within the path of your dreams.

Utilizing Social Media Platforms Like LinkedIn(Navigating the Digital Landscape for Career Success)

In ultra-modern-day digitally saturated global, social media structures like LinkedIn serve as integral gadget for young adults navigating the choppy waters of profession planning. By harnessing their power, you may enlarge your voice, broadcast your brand, and forge connections that span borders, cultures, and disciplines.

Below, we delve into the nuances of leveraging LinkedIn and other social media channels to bolster your career opportunities, garnering the eye of recruiters, hiring managers, and company heavyweights alike.

Polishing Your Profile

Your LinkedIn profile embodies your virtual man or woman, encapsulating your talents, research, and aspirations in a tidy package handy to masses and thousands worldwide. Invest effort and time in crafting an fascinating profile that commands attention, elicits intrigue, and invitations engagement.

Optimize your headline, juxtaposing key phrases that replicate your statistics, targets, or place of hobby. Compose a succinct, attractive summary that distills your essence, tantalizing web site site visitors with glimpses of your accomplishments, ability, and allure.

Populate your experience section with bullet factors that trumpet your achievements, quantifying your impacts whenever feasible. Solicit endorsements and hints from colleagues, supervisors, or mentors who can vouchsafe your competence, credibility, and individual.

Curate a medley of multimedia content material cloth that showcases your prowess, setting movies, slide decks, or weblog posts that add texture, intensity, and size for your profile. Publish lengthy-form articles that feature you as a idea leader, organising on trending topics or arguable problems that ignite passionate debates.

Expanding Your Network

LinkedIn's algorithm prioritizes connections, raising profiles that boast expansive networks populated with the aid of the usage of diverse, excessive-profile people. Actively are looking for like-minded experts, becoming a member of companies that align collectively together with your pastimes, values, or objectives.

Attend virtual sports, webinars, or hangouts that foster interactions, forging connections that circulate beyond our on-line world. Engage in conversations that meander off script, traversing uncharted territories that challenge conventional statistics and defy orthodoxy.

Leverage your alma mater's alumni database, mining it for nuggets of gold that gleam with capability. Cold-message strangers who pique your interest, providing informational interviews that monitor you to novel thoughts, perspectives, or paradigms.

Participating in Groups and Discussions

Groups and discussions offer fertile grounds for sowing seeds that flower into relationships, binding you to kindred spirits who percentage your passions, obsessions, or fixations. Contributions that resonate with company individuals vault you into the limelight, burnishing your popularity and cementing your reputation as a valued participant.

Monitor threads that ignite your interest, chiming in with comments that upload fee, inject levity, or provoke notion. Share content that resonates collectively along with your tribe, tagging influencers who might probably respect your curation.

Posting Content Regularly

Content consumption consumes limitless hours, commanding center diploma in our fractured hobby economic gadget. Produce chunk-sized morsels that satisfy appetites for records, enjoyment, or escapism.

Curate articles, memes, or films that tickle your fancy, disseminating them for the duration of systems that cater to diverse tastes, alternatives, or proclivities. Infuse your musings with character, humanity, and soul, rendering them impossible to face as much as to clients hungry for substance, style, or panache.

Chapter 6: Mastering Interview Skills

A Crucial Step towards Career Success for Young Adults

Landing an interview marks a momentous milestone to your career adventure, heralding opportunities to showcase your capability, charm interviewers, and clinch coveted interest gives. Yet, interviews pose formidable annoying conditions, exacting tolls on nerves, self belief, or composure.

Honed interview abilities represent a thriller weapon that stages the playing situation, permitting you to shine brightly, radiate air of mystery, and dazzle assessors. Developing the ones competencies calls for aware attempt, strategic making plans, and perseverance.

Below, we delve into the nuances of interview abilities, equipping you with insights, techniques, and examples that catapult you toward achievement.

Understanding Interview Basics

Interviews serve a couple of purposes, starting from evaluating candidates' qualifications, cultural fits, or motivations to dispelling doubts, clarifying misunderstandings, or negotiating terms. They expect diverse formats, from one-on-one sit down-downs, panel discussions, or company sports activities to video calls, telephone chats, or simulations.

Preparation proves pivotal, concerning coming across businesses, merchandise, or services that pique your hobby. Familiarize your self with interviewers' backgrounds, accomplishments, or pursuits, unearthing commonalities that foster rapport.

Anticipate likely questions, rehearsing responses that display off your acumen, resourcefulness, or adaptability. Concoct anecdotes that dramatize your achievements, illustrating your prowess, resilience, or creativity.

Displaying Professionalism and Poise

First impressions rely, putting the tone for subsequent interactions. Dress well, groom impeccably, and behave in a well mannered way, exuding an air of calm, accrued self notion.

Greet interviewers warmly, shaking arms firmly, making eye contact, and smiling virtually. Display lively listening abilties, leaning barely ahead, nodding now and again, and paraphrasing key points.

Articulate your thoughts sincerely, coherently, and succinctly, pausing periodically to accumulate your mind or invite questions. Exhibit enthusiasm, interest, or passion, betraying your zest for mastering, growing, or contributing.

Answering Questions Effectively

Question-and-answer schooling shape the spine of interviews, disturbing deft maneuvering, astute calculations, and measured responses. Handle curveballs deftly, defusing anxiety, neutralizing hostility, or salvaging dignity.

Address every query proper away, fending off tangents, diversions, or equivocations. Structure your replies logically, sequentially, and persuasively, buttressing claims with proof, reasoning, or examples.

Counter negativity, defensiveness, or aggression with positivity, openness, or empathy, diffusing confrontations or preserving off escalations. Manifest humility, teachability, or vulnerability, confessing lack of records, acknowledging mistakes, or soliciting remarks.

Posing Insightful Questions

Questions recommend your engagement, interest, or initiative, revealing your intellect, instinct, or instincts. Query interviewers about their roles, responsibilities, or stressful conditions, eliciting insights, warfare tales, or know-how.

Inquire approximately agency techniques, marketplace dispositions, or organization shifts, betokening your industrial acumen, strategic thinking, or visionary streak. Challenge assumptions, biases, or dogmas, displaying your courage, conviction, or contrarianism.

Negotiating Terms

Salary negotiations constitute a touchy dance, requiring worldwide family contributors, tact, and flexibility. Research remuneration packages, armed with facts, comparisons, or benchmarks that bolster your bargaining power.

Justify your wishes, bringing up accomplishments, contributions, or capability that warrant fees, incentives, or rewards. Counteroffer tactfully, conceding gracefully, or compromising shrewdly, retaining relationships, reputations, or alternatives.

In end, mastering interview abilties represents a critical step in the direction of career achievement for teenagers. By internalizing those requirements, operating in the direction of diligently, and studying from actual-life examples, you could ace interviews, bag gives, and kickstart your expert odyssey.

Preparing for Behavioral and Situational Interview Questions

Preparing for behavioral and situational interview questions is an critical element of career making plans for teenagers. These varieties of questions aim to assess your hassle-fixing talents, adaptability, and potential to deal with actual-life situations inside the place of business. Here's a entire communicate on a way to prepare for behavioral and situational interview questions:

Understanding Behavioral and Situational Interview Questions:

Behavioral interview questions ask applicants to provide an explanation for beyond opinions and the way they handled specific situations. These questions typically start with phrases which embody "Tell me approximately a time at the same time as..." or "Describe a situation wherein..." The concept at the back of behavioral interview questions is that beyond conduct predicts future ordinary overall performance.

Situational interview questions, however, present hypothetical conditions and ask applicants how they may reply. These questions usually start with terms along with "What may want to you do if..." or "How could you manage..." Situational interview questions investigate a candidate's important questioning and desire-making skills.

Analyzing the Job Description:

To prepare for behavioral and situational interview questions, begin via analyzing the project description. Identify the key competencies and abilities required for the mission and remember examples from your past reviews that show off these abilties.

Consider situations in that you confronted demanding situations, made difficult picks, or confirmed control.

Using the STAR Method

The STAR technique is a useful framework for answering behavioral interview questions. STAR stands for Situation, Task, Action, Result. Describe the Situation or Task, give an cause of the Action you took, and proportion the Results of your moves. Using the STAR approach ensures that you provide an entire and concise answer that demonstrates your skills and capabilities.

Preparing Stories

Prepare numerous recollections that exhibit your abilities and research. Choose recollections that show off your hassle-fixing capabilities, manipulate skills, teamwork, and versatility. Make positive your memories are relevant to the interest and the agency. Practice telling your memories out loud, so you come to be cushty relaying them throughout the interview.

Anticipating Situational Questions

Try to count on situational interview questions based totally at the pastime description and the business enterprise. Think about how you can address not unusual situations within the employer or place of job. Practice your responses out loud, so that you revel in assured and prepared in a few unspecified time in the destiny of the interview.

Responding to Behavioral and Situational Questions

When answering behavioral and situational interview questions, be particular and concise. Use the STAR approach to structure your answers and provide concrete examples. Avoid the usage of generalizations or hypotheticals. Instead, interest for your past studies and the manner they relate to the approach and the organization.

Common Behavioral and Situational Interview Questions:

Here are some not unusual behavioral and situational interview questions:

Tell me approximately a time while you had to deal with a tough coworker.

Describe a situation in that you needed to remedy a complex problem.

What may want to you do if you disagreed with your boss's desire?

How may additionally you address a situation in which you unnoticed a vital reduce-off date?

Describe a time on the equal time as you had to lead a set to complete a venture.

What may you do if you located a colleague violating corporation insurance?

In stop, getting prepared for behavioral and situational interview questions is important for career making plans achievement. By understanding the types of questions, reading the project description, the usage of the STAR approach, making ready recollections, and schooling your responses, you could monitor your abilities and abilties to functionality employers. Remember to be precise, concise, and relevant to your solutions, and you'll increase your possibilities of landing the interest.

Dressing Appropriately and Making a Strong First Impression

First impressions count number, specifically in the expert global. Dressing appropriately and making a strong first impact can significantly impact your profession potentialities. In this section, we are succesful to talk about the significance of dressing effectively and offer tips on creating a first rate first affect.

Why Dressing Appropriately Matters

Dressing correctly for an event or place of job sends a message about your professionalism, interest to element, and respect for the surroundings you are in. It allows you healthy in, establishes credibility, and makes a announcement about your man or woman and paintings ethic. Moreover, dressing because it need to be can also growth yourself perception and assist you experience more focused and professional.

Understanding Dress Codes

Different workplaces and industries have wonderful dress codes. Understanding the get dressed code of a workplace can help you decide what to position on and make a excellent first affect. Here are some common dress codes:

Business formal: This is the most formal dress code, typically worn in law firms, banking institutions, and distinct expert settings. Men commonly placed on suits, ties, and dress footwear, whilst girls wear fits, garments, or skirts with blouses and heels.

Business informal: This get dressed code is commonplace in workplaces and allows for additonal comfortable clothing. Men can placed on slacks, polo shirts, and dress footwear, on the equal time as girls can put on blouses, skirts, or pants with dress shoes or houses. Jeans, sneakers, and T-shirts are typically not proper.

Casual: This dress code is becoming extra not unusual in startups and innovative industries. It permits for added comfortable garb, in conjunction with denims, T-shirts, and shoes. However, it is nonetheless vital to keep a expert look and keep away from carrying overly informal garments, together with shorts or turn-flops.

Tips for Dressing Appropriately

Here are some guidelines for dressing successfully in a professional setting:

Research the employer way of life and get dressed code earlier than your interview or first day of labor.

Choose clothes that healthy nicely and are snug to put on.

Opt for unbiased shades, which include black, military, grey, or brown, which may be considered expert and bendy.

Accessorize conservatively, together with with an eye fixed constant, belt, or jewelry.

Iron or steam your garments before carrying them to avoid wrinkles.

Keep make-up and fragrances to a minimal.

Making a Strong First Impression

Making a strong first have an effect on is going past dressing as it should be. Here are some pointers for making a outstanding first effect:

Arrive early: Arriving early indicates which you are punctual, reliable, and respectful of various people's time.

Greet human beings warmly: Smiling, making eye contact, and shaking arms can help installation a pleasant and professional surroundings.

Show enthusiasm: Expressing hobby and enthusiasm for the method and organization can assist monitor your motivation and strength of mind.

Listen actively: Paying interest to what others say and displaying that you rate their evaluations can assist assemble rapport and believe.

Ask questions: Asking considerate questions can display that you are curious, concerned, and engaged.

Chapter 7: Entrepreneurship

Entrepreneurship has emerged as a promising and profitable profession course for teenagers who aspire to break free from traditional employment models and create their very own possibilities. With the upward thrust of generation and the internet, starting a commercial corporation has turn out to be less complex and further less costly than ever earlier than. However, entrepreneurship is not for the faint-hearted. It calls for grit, determination, and a willingness to take dangers.

Young entrepreneurs face unique disturbing conditions, along with confined experience, assets, and networks. Nevertheless, further they private superb benefits, collectively with younger electricity, creativity, and versatility. As such, it is vital to provide teenagers with the gear, expertise, and assets needed to prevail within the global of entrepreneurship.

This segment explores the concept of entrepreneurship as a possible career direction for teens. It covers different factors of entrepreneurship, which include ideation, validation, investment, scaling, and exit technique. Through actual-global examples, case research, and expert insights, this phase dreams to empower young adults with the self perception and abilities wished to expose their entrepreneurial desires proper proper into a truth.

Whether you are a pupil seeking to begin a facet hustle or a more younger expert on the lookout for to launch a complete-scale undertaking, this phase gives treasured insights and sensible advice for every degree of the entrepreneurial adventure. So, buckle up and be a part of us as we delve into the thrilling global of entrepreneurship.

Entrepreneurship has end up an more and more famous career path for young adults seeking out autonomy, creativity, and monetary freedom. Launching a successful project calls for cautious planning, studies, and execution. In this text, we're capable of discover 3 important steps for teenagers interested by pursuing entrepreneurship: figuring out business organization thoughts that align with passions and competencies, wearing out marketplace studies and growing a business plan, and financing and launching your own assignment.

Identifying Business Ideas That Align with Passions and Skills

Starting a commercial enterprise enterprise may be a tough and profitable experience. One of the keys to success is identifying a business company idea that aligns together with your passions and capabilities. To do that, you could have a look at those steps:

Reflect for your pursuits, hobbies, and values. Consider what you revel in doing for your loose time, what issues you're enthusiastic about fixing, and what values are essential to you.

Examine your strengths and weaknesses. Identify the skills and know-how you have obtained via education, work experience, or private tasks. Determine which skills are transferable to entrepreneurship and which of them you need to accumulate or enhance.

Brainstorm thoughts that combine your passions and talents. Generate a listing of capacity organizations that align alongside facet your pastimes and strengths. Consider the dimensions of the marketplace, opposition, scalability, and profitability.

Test your mind with buddies, own family, or potential customers. Get comments on your mind, validate your assumptions, and refine your pitch.

Let's take a look at Sarah's case. She is a current university graduate, loves photos and traveling. She comes to a selection to begin a pics business agency that makes a speciality of taking images memorable moments at some point of journeys and adventures. Her ardour for pictures and adventure lets in her to create a completely precise and attractive product that resonates along side her goal market.

Conducting Market Research and Creating a Business Plan

Market research is a essential step inside the entrepreneurial approach. It includes amassing and analyzing data about your competitors, customers, and market conditions. Based for your findings, you can create a marketing strategy that outlines your imaginative and prescient, challenge, desires, strategies, and techniques. Here are some recommendations for wearing out market studies and developing a marketing and advertising and marketing method:

Define your goal market. Identify the demographics, psychographics, and pain factors of your excellent patron.

Study your opposition. Analyze their strengths, weaknesses, pricing, distribution channels, and marketing strategies.

Collect facts from number one and secondary sources. Primary property embody surveys, interviews, and observations. Secondary resources embody authorities databases, enterprise reports, and academic research.

Validate your assumptions. Test your hypotheses about your product, fee, placement, and advertising.

Develop a SWOT evaluation. Identify your strengths, weaknesses, possibilities, and threats.

Set measurable desires and KPIs. Determine how you may diploma your development and success.

John, a computer era number one, desires to create a cell app that streamlines the ordering machine for ingesting places. He conducts market studies and discovers that the food transport market is pretty aggressive, with installation gamers which encompass DoorDash and UberEats dominating the marketplace. However, he furthermore identifies an opening in the marketplace for a cost-effective solution for impartial eating locations. He creates a advertising strategy that consists of an intensive description of his product, pricing version, marketing strategy, and monetary projections.

Financing and Launching Your Own Venture:

Launching a commercial enterprise calls for capital, property, and operational assist. There are numerous methods to finance your undertaking, which incorporates bootstrapping, crowdfunding, angel buyers, mission capital, and loans. Here are some suggestions for financing and launching your very personal venture:

Bootstrap your commercial enterprise organisation. Use your financial monetary savings, credit score score cards, or income out of your day technique to fund your startup.

Crowdfund your venture. Raise price range from a big style of humans thru structures which consist of Kickstarter or Indiegogo.

Pitch to angel consumers or assignment capitalists. Present your marketing approach to potential shoppers who can provide investment and mentorship.

Apply for loans or presents. Explore federal, country, or community applications that provide financing or subsidies for small companies.

Build a lean startup. Focus on growing a minimum viable product (MVP) that meets the easy desires of your customers. Iterate and enhance primarily based on comments and information.

Hire a skilled group. Recruit personnel or contractors who complement your competencies and percentage your vision.

Chapter 8: Continuing Education And Professional Development

Continuing training and professional improvement are crucial factors of profession making plans for young adults. With rapidly evolving technology, transferring mission markets, and elevated international competition, staying current with the present day-day knowledge and capabilities is essential for profession development and fulfillment.

Continuing schooling refers to any educational sports activities undertaken after excessive college or university, which includes certificates programs, workshops, seminars, and superior levels. Professional development, but, refers to the manner of improving one's skills, knowledge, and talents in a specific profession or career.

Both persevering with training and expert improvement provide severa advantages, collectively with progressed employability, higher earning capacity, superior system safety, and extended assignment delight. Moreover, they allow individuals to stay aggressive in their respective fields, expand their professional networks, and benefit recognition and credibility in their careers.

Despite the ones blessings, many teens overlook the significance of persevering with training and expert improvement in their career making plans efforts. According to a survey through the American Society for Training and Development, best 38% of employees get keep of formal education from their employers, even as handiest 25% participate in out of doors training or education applications.

To address this hollow, this phase gives valuable insights and updated information on continuing schooling and professional development as part of a profession making plans guide for young adults. Whether you're a present day graduate, a more younger expert, or someone trying to transfer careers, this phase will help you apprehend the importance of lifelong studying, find out possibilities for persevering with education and professional development, and increase a plan to attain your career dreams.

We will communicate the severa styles of continuing schooling and professional development, together with certificate, workshops, seminars, and superior stages, and the benefits and downsides of each. We can absolutely have a look at the awesome strategies of obtaining continuing education credit, collectively with on line courses, distance getting to know, and self-observe, and the factors to recall whilst deciding on a continuing schooling corporation.

Additionally, we're able to provide recommendations and strategies for developing a non-save you learning plan, putting mastering desires, and measuring development, as well as actual-worldwide examples of people who have successfully integrated continuing education and expert development into their careers.

By the surrender of this section, you can have a higher information of the significance of continuing schooling and expert improvement in profession planning, and be prepared with the information and competencies to create a plan for lifelong getting to know and profession boom.

Pursuing Advanced Degrees or Certifications

Pursuing superior stages or certifications can substantially beautify your career prospects, in particular in fields that require specialised understanding and information. Obtaining an advanced degree or certification can bring about better salaries, greater mission protection, and multiplied opportunities for career improvement. However, it's important to weigh the blessings towards the prices, as advanced degrees and certifications can be luxurious and time-ingesting to gather.

When thinking about whether or now not to pursue a sophisticated diploma or certification, right right here are a few key elements to keep in mind:

Relevance for your career dreams. Does the advanced degree or certification align on the side of your lengthy-time period profession aspirations? Will it offer you with the competencies and understanding crucial to reap your selected area? It's important to pick out a software program software to help you obtain your specific career dreams.

Cost. Advanced degrees and certifications may be pricey, starting from masses to tens of plenty of dollars. Consider whether or not or now not or now not the rate of this device is justified by way of way of manner of the potential income increase and profession development opportunities it is able to provide. Look into monetary beneficial aid options, together with scholarships, offers, and loans, to help offset the charge.

Time willpower. Obtaining a complicated diploma or certification can take everywhere from several months to severa years, depending on the software program application and it slow table. Consider whether or not or not you've got the time and bandwidth to determine to a rigorous academic application at the same time as additionally balancing exclusive responsibilities, collectively with artwork and family.

ROI. Return on funding (ROI) is an important element to don't forget while identifying whether or not or no longer to pursue a complicated degree or certification. Consider the functionality income growth and career development opportunities the diploma or certification can also need to provide, and take a look at that to the price and time willpower required to advantage it.

Employer useful resource. Some employers provide training help or repayment for personnel who pursue advanced stages or certifications associated with their approach. Check collectively together with your company to look in the event that they offer this form of programs, and whether or not or not they is probably inclined to help your pursuit of a sophisticated diploma or certification.

Program excellent. It's critical to select a extraordinary software that allows you to provide you with the competencies and statistics critical to acquire your selected issue. Research one-of-a-kind applications and faculties, and look for accreditation, ratings, and critiques from authentic resources.

Some popular superior stages and certifications for teenagers include:

Master's Degree: A draw close's degree is a sophisticated degree that commonly calls for 2 years of entire-time observe beyond a bachelor's diploma. Popular draw near's tiers for young adults embody the ones in employer management (MBA), engineering, training, and healthcare.

Doctoral Degree: A doctoral degree is the very high-quality diploma of tutorial diploma, and commonly calls for 4 to 6 years of complete-time observe beyond a bachelor's diploma. Popular doctoral levels for teens encompass those in remedy (MD), law (JD), psychology, and physics.

Certified Public Accountant (CPA): A CPA is an authorized professional accountant who has passed a rigorous exam administered thru the American Institute of Certified Public Accountants (AICPA). CPAs are in excessive demand in the accounting and finance industries, and generally earn better salaries than non-licensed accountants.

Project Management Professional (PMP): A PMP is an authorized professional challenge supervisor who has tested know-how in task manipulate first-rate practices. PMPs are in excessive name for in a number of industries, along with production, IT, and production.

Certified Information Systems Security Professional (CISSP): A CISSP is an authorized cybersecurity expert who has set up know-how in shielding virtual property and infrastructure. CISSPs are in excessive name for within the generation and safety industries.

Ultimately, pursuing a complex degree or certification can be a sensible investment to your destiny profession opportunities. However, it's important to carefully have a study the prices and advantages, and choose out a software program software that aligns together together with your lengthy-term career goals.

Keeping up with Industry Trends and Best Practices

Let's dive into the subject of preserving up with business enterprise tendencies and superb practices because it pertains to career planning for teens.

Importance of Staying Current

Industries are continuously changing, with new improvements, technology, and dispositions developing often. Staying modern-day-day with the ones modifications is important for profession fulfillment, because it allows humans to stay competitive and relevant in their fields. By keeping up with enterprise tendencies and high-quality practices, teenagers can function themselves as informed and succesful experts who're able to adapt to changing instances and deliver amazing artwork.

Ways to Stay Updated

There are severa techniques that teens can live up to date on enterprise tendencies and brilliant practices. Here are some hints:

Read Industry News: Subscribing to enterprise courses or blogs can assist human beings stay informed about the extraordinarily-modern developments of their fields. For example, advertising and marketing and advertising and marketing specialists could possibly join Adweek or Hubspot, at the same time as engineers may additionally have a look at Engineering.Com or IEEE Spectrum.

Attend Conferences and Workshops: Attending conferences and workshops is a superb manner to hook up with other specialists for your region and discover about new traits and excellent practices. Many conferences provide keynote speeches, panel discussions, and interactive workshops that would assist human beings amplify their information and skillsets.

Follow Thought Leaders: Following influential idea leaders for your company can help you stay up to date on the cutting-edge day traits and remarkable practices. Many concept leaders percentage their insights and knowledge on social media structures which incorporates Twitter or LinkedIn.

Join Professional Associations: Joining expert establishments can offer individuals with access to valuable belongings, together with employer studies, networking opportunities, and education applications. Many institutions moreover provide webinars, newsletters, and unique materials that could assist humans live informed about the modern-day trends and tremendous practices.

Participate in Online Communities: Participating in online agencies, consisting of boards or speak agencies, can help humans hook up with specific professionals in their fields and live knowledgeable about the modern developments and tremendous practices. Reddit, Quora, and Stack Exchange are all famous systems for on line corporations.

Benefits of Staying Current

Staying modern with business organization developments and brilliant practices may want to have severa blessings for teenagers. Here are a number of the maximum excellent:

Competitive Advantage: Staying up to date on organization traits and excellent practices can deliver human beings a aggressive advantage inside the technique marketplace. Employers rate applicants who're knowledgeable approximately the extremely-cutting-edge trends and technology, and are more likely to rent people who are in a position to reveal their understanding.

Chapter 9: Coping With Setbacks And Challenges

Coping with setbacks and traumatic conditions is an inevitable a part of any career adventure. Even with careful making plans and education, sudden boundaries can stand up, leaving young adults feeling discouraged, defeated, or uncertain about their futures. However, setbacks and demanding situations also can be transformative reports that foster resilience, increase, and self-discovery. In this phase, we are in a position to speak coping mechanisms and techniques for managing setbacks and challenges as they relate to career planning for young adults.

Setbacks and worrying situations can take many forms, from activity loss, rejection, and failure to discrimination, harassment, and trauma. Whatever the individual of the setback or venture, it's far important to widely recognized and validate the emotional response it elicits. Suppressing or denying feelings of anger, frustration, disappointment, or unhappiness can restrict recovery and increase, prolonging the healing machine and perpetuating bad forms of wondering and behaving. Accepting and processing feelings in a wholesome and positive way is critical for retaining intellectual and emotional health, restoring equilibrium, and moving in advance with reason and cause.

Coping mechanisms and strategies for handling setbacks and demanding situations variety depending on the individual, the severity of the setback or undertaking, and the to be had assets and assist structures. Some not unusual coping mechanisms embody looking for social useful useful resource, working toward self-care, reframing bad mind, and setting sensible dreams.

Seeking social guide includes confiding in trusted pals, family individuals, or specialists approximately the setback or mission. Sharing evaluations, feelings, and worries with others can provide comfort, reassurance, and mindset, supporting people realize they're not on my own in their struggles. Social assist can also facilitate hassle-solving, brainstorming, and networking, taking off up new opportunities and opportunities.

Practicing self-care involves carrying out sports that sell rest, restoration, and rejuvenation. Self-care practices can variety from meditation, yoga, workout, and journaling to hobbies, entertainment sports, and modern pastimes. Self-care is crucial for maintaining bodily, highbrow, and emotional fitness, enhancing resilience, and promoting everyday fitness.

Reframing horrible mind consists of recognizing and hard restricting ideals, cognitive distortions, and irrational thoughts that perpetuate awful feelings and behaviors. Reframing horrible mind includes substituting negative thoughts with top notch, empowering, and uplifting ones that foster desire, optimism, and motivation.

Setting sensible dreams consists of breaking down overwhelming or ambiguous goals into smaller, capability, and measurable steps.

Setting realistic desires includes putting in deadlines, tracking improvement, and celebrating achievements, fostering a experience of achievement, delight, and self-efficacy.

In addition to the ones coping mechanisms, searching out expert assist and assist can be instrumental in coping with setbacks and worrying conditions. Therapy, training, and counseling can offer steady, incredible, and supportive regions for exploring, addressing, and resolving non-public and expert problems. Professional assist and assist can also facilitate restoration, boom, and transformation, permitting humans to overcome obstacles, gain their dreams, and live enjoyable lives.

Real-global examples of people who've treated setbacks and disturbing conditions in their careers can encourage and inspire teens. For instance, Steve Jobs, the co-founding father of Apple Inc., became fired from the enterprise he helped create in 1985.

However, he went on to begin NeXT Computers and Pixar Animation Studios, revolutionizing the animation corporation and returning to Apple as CEO in 1997. His legacy keeps to shape the generation and layout panorama, underscoring the capability for resilience, reinvention, and redemption inside the face of adversity and defeat.

In cease, dealing with setbacks and disturbing situations is an important part of profession making plans for young adults. Acknowledging and validating feelings, searching for social help, education self-care, reframing terrible mind, and setting realistic dreams are powerful coping mechanisms and strategies for coping with setbacks and challenges. Seeking professional assist and help additionally can be instrumental in overcoming obstacles, achieving goals, and identifying aspirations. Inspiring real-global examples of people who have handled setbacks and disturbing situations can instill want, resilience, and perseverance, inspiring young adults to overcome adversity and thrive of their careers.

Life is full of united statesand downs, twists and turns. No do not forget how properly-laid our plans are, we necessarily encounter setbacks and demanding situations that threaten to derail our development and shake our self guarantee. This is mainly true inside the realm of profession making plans, in which rejection, unhappiness, and failure are all too not unusual. But whilst the ones studies may be painful and disheartening, in addition they may be effective catalysts for growth and mastering. In this text, we can find out how teenagers can deal with setbacks and demanding situations of their careers, drawing on insights from psychology, sociology, and personal development.

Handling Rejection and Disappointment

Rejection is a traditional experience, however it is able to feel notably private and devastating, in particular near our careers. Being handed over for a pastime, receiving complaint from a superior, or dropping out on a selling can purpose emotions of shame, embarrassment, and self-doubt. And because of the fact our careers are carefully tied to our identities and feel of self confidence, rejection may be specifically unfavorable to our intellectual health and nicely-being.

But whilst rejection is in no manner smooth, there are strategies to mitigate its impact and get higher more potent than in advance than. Here are some techniques for managing rejection and sadness to your profession:

Practice self-compassion: It's regular to revel in upset and upset while things do now not bypass our way, but it's far crucial to avoid beating ourselves up or falling right right into a cycle of bad self-talk. Instead, attempt to deal with yourself with kindness and compassion, honestly as you'll a near buddy or loved one. This may additionally comprise reframing the scenario in a more splendid moderate, acknowledging your strengths and accomplishments, or jogging in the direction of self-care rituals that assist you enjoy grounded and focused.

Seek support: Rejection may be separating, but it's miles important to bear in thoughts which you're not on my own. Surrounding your self with a supportive community of friends, circle of relatives individuals, or colleagues will permit you to way your emotions and advantage perspective on the state of affairs. Consider task out to a mentor or instruct who can provide steerage and encouragement, or be part of a professional association or networking enterprise employer in which you can connect with others on your location.

Learn from the revel in: Every rejection brings with it a valuable lesson, even though it's now not right now obvious. Take a while to reflect at the enjoy and understand any insights or takeaways that is probably beneficial for destiny reference. Was there a particular information or trait that held you back? Could you have furnished yourself in any other way in the interview or application way? Use this feedback to pleasant-song your method and growth your chances of achievement in the destiny.

Keep matters in mind-set: It's smooth to get caught up inside the minutiae of every day life, however it is crucial to zoom out and remind yourself of the larger photograph. Yes, rejection can sting, but it's miles not often the stop of the area. Try to keep subjects in perspective via using focusing on your prolonged-term desires and remembering that setbacks and stressful situations are a herbal part of the journey.

Learning From Failure and Using It as a Stepping Stone for Success

Failing is by no means amusing, however it's an crucial a part of growth and development. Whether it's far bombing a presentation, missing a closing date, or developing a pricey mistake, failure forces us to confront our obstacles, have a look at our assumptions, and adapt our strategies. And while it may be tempting to shrink back from threat or blame ourselves for our failures, embracing them as opportunities for learning and development can in the long run motive extra fulfillment and success.

Here are some methods to investigate from failure and use it as a stepping stone for fulfillment:

Take obligation: While it's miles critical to avoid residing on mistakes or assigning blame, it's also crucial to take responsibility for our moves and examine from them. Acknowledge the role you achieved inside the very last results, and find out any particular behaviors or selections that contributed to the failure.

Analyze the Root Cause: Dig deeper to find out the underlying motives of the failure. Were there any outside factors at play, which embody a loss of sources or conflicting priorities? Or have become the issue greater crucial, on the side of a improper method or terrible conversation?

Identify Lessons Learned: Draw insights and instructions from the enjoy at the way to will let you keep away from comparable missteps inside the destiny. This ought to possibly involve revising your approach, searching out extra schooling or help, or adjusting your expectations.

Experiment with New Approaches: Failure may be a powerful catalyst for innovation and experimentation. Use the commands determined out of your screw ups to tell your destiny experiments, and be open to new thoughts and views.

Maintaining Mental Health and Wellbeing During Stressful Times

Career planning and improvement may be fairly worthwhile, but it could additionally be fairly stressful. Between competing demands, tight time limits, and steady stress to perform, it is easy to revel in beaten and burned out. And while some pressure is everyday or perhaps beneficial, chronic pressure can take a toll on our mental health and well-being, foremost to signs inclusive of anxiety, melancholy, and burnout.

To maintain your intellectual health and well being in the course of stressful instances, do not forget the subsequent strategies:

Set practical desires: Break down huge goals into smaller, more practicable chunks, and prioritize your duties based on urgency and importance. This can help prevent overwhelm and make sure that you're making regular development toward your goals.

Establish boundaries: Protect it sluggish and energy with the beneficial aid of placing clear limitations amongst art work and private life. This may additionally include turning off e-mail notifications after hours, delegating duties to others, or saying no to non-essential commitments.

Practice self-care: Schedule everyday breaks throughout the day, have interaction in bodily hobby, and prioritize rest and rest. Taking care of your bodily health can assist enhance your mood, strength ranges, and common properly being.

Seek useful resource: Don't be afraid to reap out for assist at the same time as you want it. Talk to a relied on buddy, member of the family, or highbrow health expert about your struggles, and do not forget becoming a member of a guide group or peer community in which you may connect with others who're going via similar annoying situations.

Setbacks and challenges are an inevitable a part of any career adventure. But by way of adopting a increase attitude, looking for resource, and analyzing from our screw ups, we can flip the ones reviews into possibilities for boom and development. By prioritizing our mental fitness and fitness, we also can make certain that we are able to weather the storms of life with resilience, grit, and backbone.

Chapter 10: What Is An Apprenticeship?

An apprenticeship is a based training software program that combines classroom schooling with arms-on paintings enjoy in a specific trade or profession. It is a shape of expertise development in which humans, referred to as apprentices, examine from professional specialists in a real-international setting. Apprenticeships are normally associated with trades such as carpentry, plumbing, and electrician paintings, however in addition they exist in severa industries like healthcare, statistics technology, and finance.

Benefits of Apprenticeships:

Apprenticeships offer severa blessings for human beings looking for career improvement. Some key advantages consist of:

Practical Experience: Apprenticeships provide palms-on education, allowing human beings to apply theoretical expertise in real-global scenarios. This practical revel in enhances talents and competence in a selected vicinity.

Job Placement: Apprentices regularly have the gain of being proper now employed thru the corporation or organisation they're training with. This will boom the possibility of securing a challenge upon of completion of the apprenticeship.

Earn While You Learn: Unlike traditional education, apprenticeships provide a salary or stipend to apprentices at some point in their schooling period. This financial help allows human beings to cover their living fees on the identical time as gaining precious experience.

Industry Connections: Apprenticeships provide possibilities to network and construct relationships with specialists in the problem. These connections can be profitable while in search of destiny employment or profession advancement.

Types of Apprenticeships:

Apprenticeships are available in numerous office work, catering to splendid industries and profession paths. Some not unusual styles of apprenticeships include:

Trade Apprenticeships: These apprenticeships recognition on skilled trades which includes introduction, automobile, welding, and plumbing. Apprentices undergo fingers-on education to increase technical statistics.

Professional Apprenticeships: These apprenticeships are regularly occurring in fields like finance, facts generation, healthcare, and engineering. They combine examine room gaining knowledge of with practical enjoy, making ready individuals for expert roles.

Creative Apprenticeships: This form of apprenticeship is geared within the route of progressive industries inclusive of fashion, picture design, film manufacturing, and culinary arts. Apprentices advantage practical skills at the identical time as strolling with hooked up specialists.

Hybrid Apprenticeships: Hybrid apprenticeships combine elements of multiple disciplines, allowing human beings to expand a diverse expertise set. For example, a multimedia apprenticeship might encompass elements of graphic layout, net improvement, and video enhancing.

Apprenticeship vs. Traditional Education:

Apprenticeships range from traditional training in severa methods:

Emphasis on Practical Skills: While conventional schooling focuses on theoretical statistics, apprenticeships prioritize fingers-on experience and functionality development in a specific trade or career.

Customized Learning: Apprenticeships provide tailor-made training based totally on the character's career dreams and employer requirements. This custom designed method ensures that apprentices gather applicable abilties for their selected trouble.

Faster Entry into the Workforce: Unlike conventional education, which frequently calls for numerous years of take a look at in advance than entering into the venture marketplace, apprenticeships allow human beings to start running and earning profits at the same time as gaining knowledge of.

Industry Relevance: Apprenticeships are designed in collaboration with employer companions, making sure that the talents taught are up to date and aligned with modern-day organisation practices. This makes apprentices highly employable upon of entirety in their education.

Current Trends in Apprenticeships:

The area of apprenticeships is constantly evolving to satisfy the changing wishes of the method marketplace. Some brilliant traits encompass:

Expansion of Apprenticeships: Governments and organizations international are spotting the fee of apprenticeships and making an funding of their expansion. This has delivered approximately an increase in the availability of apprenticeship programs at some point of numerous industries.

Technological Integration: Apprenticeships are incorporating growing technology which encompass virtual reality, augmented fact, and on line gaining knowledge of structures to beautify training opinions and boom accessibility.

Diverse Apprenticeship Opportunities: Apprenticeships are growing beyond conventional trades to embody a broader type of industries. This includes sectors which includes renewable electricity, cybersecurity, digital advertising and marketing and advertising and advertising, and superior manufacturing.

Focus on Soft Skills: In addition to technical competencies, apprenticeships are setting greater emphasis on developing smooth capabilities which incorporates verbal exchange, teamwork, problem-solving, and versatility. These abilties are crucial for success in current-day expert international.

DISCOVERING YOUR INTERESTS AND SKILLS

Identifying Your Passions:

Passions are the the usage of strain inside the once more of a fulfilling and a achievement profession. To understand their passions, teenagers can do not forget the following techniques:

Reflect on Hobbies and Activities: Take inventory of sports activities that deliver satisfaction and fulfilment. Whether it's miles playing a musical device, writing, or volunteering, those sports activities can provide valuable insights into private interests.

Explore Curiosities: Pay interest to subjects, topics, or troubles that pique interest. Delve deeper into those regions thru analyzing, research, or exploration to benefit a higher information of functionality passions.

Seek Inspiration: Look for feature models or folks who inspire you. Examine their careers and the effect they've got made. This can help understand fields or industries that align with private values and pursuits.

Try New Experiences: Step from your consolation place and strive new sports or pastimes. This can assist find out hidden passions and provide a broader mind-set on potential profession paths.

Assessing Your Strengths and Weaknesses:

Understanding one's strengths and weaknesses is critical for career making plans. Here are a few strategies for assessing private strengths and weaknesses:

Self-Reflection: Take time to reflect on personal traits, abilities, and attributes. Identify regions in which you excel, which includes hassle-fixing, creativity, or control. Similarly, widely recognized areas in which improvement is wanted.

Seek Feedback: Engage in conversations with relied on mentors, instructors, or circle of relatives individuals who can provide aim remarks to your strengths and weaknesses. Their insights can offer a easy attitude and highlight areas for boom.

Personality and Aptitude Assessments: Consider taking character exams or flair checks to gain a better know-how of your natural inclinations and strengths. These exams can offer insights into potential profession paths that align on the side of your skills.

Evaluate Academic Performance: Assess your ordinary overall performance in instructional subjects to choose out regions of energy and interest. Subjects in that you excel can also moreover imply functionality career paths definitely in reality really worth exploring.

Exploring Different Career Paths:

Once teens have received clarity on their passions, pursuits, strengths, and weaknesses, it is vital to find out numerous career paths. Here are some techniques for exploring wonderful profession alternatives:

Research Occupations: Conduct studies on occupations of interest. Explore hobby descriptions, required qualifications, and functionality career development. Online sources, profession internet net web sites, and informational interviews with specialists inside the field can be valuable property of records.

Job Shadowing and Internships: Seek possibilities to shadow specialists in fields of hobby or take part in quick-term internships. This first-hand revel in gives insights into the ordinary realities of various careers.

Networking: Build a expert network via connecting with humans in industries or occupations of interest. Attend profession gala's, industry sports, or be a part of relevant professional companies. Networking can provide treasured insights, mentorship possibilities, and potential profession leads.

Volunteer Work: Engage in volunteer work related to fields of hobby. This lets in for arms-on enjoy and exposure to 1-of-a-kind artwork environments. It additionally lets in enlarge transferable abilties that may be valuable in severa profession paths.

Online Resources: Utilize on line sources like profession assessment equipment, agency-precise internet internet sites, and expert forums. These assets provide facts on particular career paths, organisation trends, and capability instructional necessities.

RESEARCHING APPRENTICESHIP OPPORTUNITIES

Once people have completed the procedure of self-exploration and recognized their profession pursuits, it is time to navigate the apprenticeship application technique. This article objectives to guide aspiring apprentices through the diverse tiers of utility, in conjunction with studying apprenticeship opportunities, making prepared software program substances, and acing the interview tool.

Researching Apprenticeship Opportunities:

Before utilising for an apprenticeship, it's miles crucial to conduct thorough studies to grow to be privy to suitable opportunities. Here are a few steps to bear in mind at some level in the research segment:

Identify Industries and Occupations: Based at the profession hobbies discovered in the route of self-exploration, slim down the industries and occupations that align with the ones interests. Consider elements collectively with hobby outlook, increase capability, and personal options.

Explore Apprenticeship Programs: Research apprenticeship applications available inside the decided on industries and occupations. Look for programs that provide entire education, reliable companions, and possibilities for career improvement.

Check Eligibility Requirements: Review the eligibility necessities for each apprenticeship software program. Ensure that you meet the age necessities, instructional qualifications, and a few exceptional prerequisites specific thru this gadget.

Research Training Providers: Investigate the education vendors associated with the apprenticeship programs of interest. Consider their reputation, track report, and the first rate of schooling they offer.

Seek Advice and Guidance: Reach out to profession counselors, mentors, or specialists in the place for advice and steering. They can provide valuable insights and tips based totally on their experience and statistics.

Preparing Application Materials:

Once suitable apprenticeship opportunities have been identified, it's far important to put together properly-crafted software program materials. Here are some key components to bear in mind:

Resume/Curriculum Vitae (CV): Create a professional resume or CV that highlights relevant competencies, evaluations, and educational records. Tailor the file to expose off how your qualifications align with the specific apprenticeship application.

Cover Letter: Craft a compelling cowl letter that expresses your interest within the apprenticeship and demonstrates your expertise of the employer. Personalize the letter for every application, addressing the ideal necessities and goals of the apprenticeship application.

Letters of Recommendation: Request letters of advice from teachers, employers, or mentors who can attest in your skills, paintings ethic, and capability. Choose people who can offer unique examples of your competencies and suitability for the apprenticeship.

Portfolio or Work Samples: If relevant, put together a portfolio or collection of work samples that display off your talents and competencies. This is mainly critical for apprenticeships in innovative fields or industries that require a tangible demonstration of abilties.

Transcripts and Certificates: Gather academic transcripts, certificate, or a few different relevant documentation that facilitates your instructional qualifications and achievements. Ensure that those files are prepared and efficaciously available for submission.

Acing the Interview Process:

Upon submission of software program materials, the next step is often an interview. Here are a few techniques that will help you excel in a few unspecified time inside the future of the interview technique:

Research the Company or Organization: Prior to the interview, thoroughly research the employer or enterprise providing the apprenticeship. Familiarize your self with their assignment, values, present day tasks, and any notable achievements. This understanding will display off your actual interest and willpower.

Practice Interview Skills: Prepare for the interview with the aid of the usage of running closer to not unusual interview questions and responses. Consider mission mock interviews with pals, own family, or career counsellors to advantage self guarantee and refine your verbal exchange skills.

Showcase Your Skills and Experience: During the interview, spotlight your applicable abilities, studies, and accomplishments. Provide specific examples that display how you have executed your abilties in actual-international situations or educational tasks.

Ask Thoughtful Questions: Prepare a listing of considerate inquiries to ask the interviewer. This indicates your enthusiasm for the apprenticeship and your choice to research greater approximately this tool and the organization. It furthermore demonstrates your proactive method to professional improvement.

Professionalism and Communication: Dress professionally for the interview and hold a excellent and confident demeanor. Practice energetic listening and effective verbal and non-verbal communication competencies. Be articulate, respectful, and attentive at some point of the interview way.

DEVELOPING ESSENTIAL SKILLS FOR SUCCESS

In extremely-contemporary aggressive hobby marketplace, proudly owning a sturdy set of skills is crucial for career achievement. While technical understanding is vital, it's miles in addition vital to expand a variety of gentle talents that decorate your commonplace expert competency. This article will discover 4 key abilities that could appreciably effect your profession trajectory: building sturdy conversation talents, developing management capabilities, enhancing essential thinking and hassle-solving abilties, and cultivating professionalism and paintings ethic. By honing the ones abilties, you can feature yourself as a valuable asset to any enterprise employer and growth your opportunities of lengthy-term fulfillment.

Building Strong Communication Skills

Effective verbal exchange is the cornerstone of professional success, permitting you to articulate thoughts, construct relationships, and collaborate successfully. Here are a few strategies to assemble robust communication abilties:

Active Listening: Practice lively listening with the aid of giving your complete interest to the speaker, preserving eye touch, and keeping off interruptions. Summarize and ask clarifying inquiries to ensure an in depth facts of the message being conveyed.

Verbal and Written Communication: Develop easy and concise verbal and written verbal exchange competencies. Express your mind articulately, use appropriate language, and tailor your message to the meant target audience. Pay interest to grammar, spelling, and punctuation in written communique.

Nonverbal Communication: Understand the strength of nonverbal cues, along with body language, facial expressions, and tone of voice. Be aware of your non-public nonverbal communication and interpret others' nonverbal cues because it ought to be to build rapport and avoid misunderstandings.

Empathy and Emotional Intelligence: Cultivate empathy and emotional intelligence to understand and hook up with others on a deeper degree. Consider one in every of a type perspectives, show empathy toward colleagues and clients, and adapt your verbal exchange fashion to house various personalities and cultural backgrounds.

Conflict Resolution: Develop abilities in dealing with conflicts and resolving place of business disagreements. Learn to take note of precise viewpoints, are in search of for common ground, and negotiate answers that satisfy all activities concerned. Effective conflict decision fosters a fine paintings surroundings and strengthens expert relationships.

Presentation Skills: Enhance your presentation abilties through way of organizing your mind, growing attractive visible aids, and operating in the direction of powerful delivery. Utilize storytelling strategies, talk with self notion, and have interaction the goal market to maintain your message persuasively.

Developing Leadership Abilities

Leadership capabilities are especially valued within the place of work, regardless of your role. Developing these talents will can help you encourage and inspire others, strain alternate, and address extra obligations. Consider the subsequent techniques to increase your manage competencies:

Self-Awareness: Reflect on your strengths, weaknesses, and management fashion. Identify areas for development and are attempting to find remarks from mentors or colleagues. Understanding yourself better will assist you lead with authenticity and adapt your leadership approach to first rate conditions.

Effective Communication: As a leader, effective communique is paramount. Clearly articulate your imaginative and prescient, goals, and expectancies in your organisation. Be open to comments, inspire collaboration, and foster a manner of life of transparency and trust.

Decision-Making: Hone your preference-making talents via amassing relevant facts, reading facts, and thinking about the capability impact of your alternatives. Practice making options in a well timed way at the same time as balancing risks and benefits. Learn from each successes and screw ups to refine your choice-making competencies.

Delegation and Empowerment: Learn to delegate obligations efficiently, matching the right people with the right responsibilities. Empower your crew members with the aid of supplying them with the crucial assets, aid, and autonomy to excel in their roles. Trust their skills and offer guidance at the same time as wanted.

Conflict Resolution and Problem Solving: Leaders regularly come upon conflicts and complex problems. Develop your skills in resolving conflicts and locating revolutionary answers. Encourage open talk, mediate conflicts, and foster a hassle-fixing mind-set inner your crew.

Continuous Learning: Leadership is a lifelong journey of getting to know and boom. Seek opportunities to increase your statistics and skills via workshops, seminars, books, or online publications. Stay knowledgeable about industry dispositions and outstanding practices to manual your group effectively.

Enhancing Critical Thinking and Problem-Solving Skills

In modern-day dynamic and rapid-paced paintings environments, the capability to suppose considerably and clear up problems correctly is highly valued. Here are a few techniques to enhance your critical wondering and trouble-fixing competencies:

Analytical Thinking: Develop your analytical talents to break down complicated problems into viable additives. Gather relevant records, examine precise views, and choose out styles and developments. Apply logical reasoning to reach at properly-informed selections.

Creativity and Innovation: Cultivate your modern questioning talents to generate sparkling thoughts and cutting-edge solutions. Embrace a boom mind-set, undertaking assumptions, and find out new strategies to hassle-fixing. Encourage brainstorming and collaboration within your crew to foster a subculture of creativity.

Data Analysis: Enhance your capacity to research and interpret information. Learn to apply information visualization device, statistical evaluation strategies, and information-pushed desire-making methodologies. Use facts to aid your arguments, find out dispositions, and make informed choices.

Adaptability: Develop adaptability capabilities to navigate via changeand uncertainty. Be open to new thoughts and views, and encompass disturbing situations as opportunities for growth. Adapt your problem-solving technique even as confronted with unexpected obstacles or shifting priorities.

Systematic Approach: Adopt a scientific method to trouble-solving thru defining the problem really, gathering applicable statistics, generating capability solutions, evaluating their feasibility, and imposing the most viable choice. Consider the functionality risks and benefits related to every answer.

Collaboration: Recognize the rate of collaboration in trouble-solving. Seek enter from numerous views and leverage the collective intelligence of your crew. Encourage open conversation and create an environment wherein every body feels comfortable sharing their ideas and insights.

Cultivating Professionalism and Work Ethic

Cultivating professionalism and a strong artwork ethic is important for constructing a successful and fascinating career. Here are a few methods to cultivate professionalism and artwork ethic:

Reliability and Accountability: Demonstrate reliability by means of using amusing your commitments and assembly time limits continuously. Take ownership of your actions and be accountable for your art work and its results. Be proactive in locating solutions to challenges and take initiative to make contributions beyond your assigned obligations.

Time Management: Master the paintings of time control to optimize productivity and meet cut-off dates. Prioritize obligations, create a time table, and remove distractions. Learn to balance competing priorities and allocate time correctly to make certain properly timed delivery of tremendous work.

Adaptability and Flexibility: Embrace change and display screen adaptability in the face of evolving situations. Be open to new thoughts, approaches, and technology. Show flexibility in adjusting to new roles, obligations, and artwork environments.

Professional Etiquette: Develop sturdy expert etiquette thru adhering to place of business norms and displaying apprehend within the path of co-employees, clients, and superiors. Maintain a expert appearance and communicate professionally in all interactions, each in man or woman and on-line.

Continuous Learning and Development: Commit to continuous gaining knowledge of and professional development. Stay updated on enterprise trends, era, and notable practices. Seek possibilities for education, certifications, and capacity enhancement to stay in advance to your challenge.

Ethical Conduct: Uphold immoderate ethical necessities in all components of your art work. Act with integrity, preserve confidentiality whilst required, and keep away from conflicts of interest. Make moral picks that align collectively collectively together with your values and the ideas of your business enterprise.

APPLYING FOR APPRENTICESHIPS

Completing your apprenticeship is a huge milestone for your professional adventure. As you close to the surrender of this phase, it is crucial to begin planning your transition to complete-time employment. This article will guide you via the gadget, which include assessing your options, making prepared for the interest searching for, acing interviews, and negotiating procedure gives. By following those steps, you can effortlessly navigate the transition and set yourself up for achievement in your preferred profession route.

Assessing Your Options

Before launching into the mission seek, make an effort to assess your alternatives and align them collectively with your profession dreams. Here's how you may compare your opportunities:

Reflect on Your Apprenticeship Experience: Consider the capabilities, knowledge, and reviews obtained within the path of your apprenticeship. Assess how the ones align together together with your extended-time period career desires and the unique industries or roles you're interested by pursuing.

Evaluate Internal Opportunities: Explore whether or not or not your current-day organisation gives any inner undertaking possibilities or pathways for boom. Speak collectively at the side of your manager or mentor to recognize the possibilities in the organisation.

Research External Opportunities: Conduct entire research on assignment marketplace trends, industries, and corporations of interest. Identify ability employers who value apprenticeship enjoy and offer possibilities for career improvement.

Networking and Informational Interviews: Leverage your professional community and behavior informational interviews with specialists to your favored industries or roles. Seek their insights on functionality profession paths, enterprise tendencies, and to be had opportunities.

Consider Further Education: Assess whether or not additional schooling or certifications may beautify your qualifications and open doors to more appropriate positions. Determine if pursuing higher training aligns together with your profession goals and if it's going to offer a competitive gain in your preferred subject.

Acing the Job Interview

Once you stable device interviews, it is essential to put together and present your self effectively. Here are some recommendations that will help you ace the interview:

Research the Company: Thoroughly studies the corporation company in advance than the interview. Understand their undertaking, values, current initiatives, and any giant achievements. This understanding will display your proper hobby and preparedness.

Practice Common Interview Questions: Prepare responses to common interview questions, along side those associated with your apprenticeship revel in, strengths and weaknesses, and problem-fixing abilities. Practice with a chum or member of the family to refine your answers.

Showcase Your Apprenticeship Experience: Highlight the talents, understanding, and achievements obtained within the route of your apprenticeship. Provide precise examples that screen how you've got applied your capabilities in actual-worldwide conditions. Illustrate your adaptability, teamwork, and willpower to getting to know.

Communicate Effectively: During the interview, talk virtually and hopefully. Use energetic listening capabilities to surely understand the questions earlier than presenting considerate and concise responses. Maintain suitable eye contact and show excellent body language.

Ask Relevant Questions: Prepare a listing of questions to ask the interviewer. Inquire approximately the organization manner of lifestyles, boom possibilities, or particular tasks you may be worried in. Thoughtful questions display your enthusiasm and engagement inside the communication.

Follow-Up with a Thank-You Note: After each interview, deliver a custom designed thank-you phrase to the interviewer expressing your gratitude for the opportunity. Reiterate your hobby in the role and in brief summarize why you don't forget you are a robust in shape.

Negotiating Job Offers

When to procure a hobby provide, it is vital to barter phrases that align together along with your expectations and goals. Here's how you could method the negotiation way:

Assess the Offer: Carefully assessment the undertaking offer, thinking about factors together with earnings, advantages, task responsibilities, and increase possibilities. Compare the offer collectively collectively along with your research on enterprise requirements and not unusual salaries for comparable positions.

Prepare for Negotiation: Determine your chosen profits variety and be prepared to articulate your rate continued:

Prepare for Negotiation: Determine your preferred profits range and be prepared to articulate your price to the commercial enterprise business enterprise. Consider different factors of the offer that can be negotiable, along side tour time, professional improvement possibilities, or bendy paintings arrangements.

Justify Your Request: When negotiating, provide easy and compelling reasons why you deserve a better earnings or additional benefits. Highlight your applicable competencies, enjoy, and the charge you can deliver to the enterprise enterprise. Emphasize your accomplishments inside the route of your apprenticeship and the way they align with the characteristic you are being provided.

Maintain Professionalism: Approach the negotiation procedure with professionalism and appreciate. Be confident but now not confrontational. Remember that negotiations are a collaborative method geared toward locating a together beneficial agreement.

Consider Trade-Offs: Be open to change-offs or opportunity solutions if the preliminary provide can't be met in its entirety. For instance, if the sales can not be extended, you may negotiate for delivered holiday days or a flexible work time table.

Get It in Writing: Once an agreement is reached, make certain that each one agreed-upon terms are documented in writing. Review the activity offer letter or agreement carefully to affirm that it efficiently displays the negotiated phrases.

MAKING THE MOST OF YOUR APPRENTICESHIP

Congratulations on securing an entire-time function! As you embark on your professional adventure, it's far essential to prioritize your ongoing development to thrive in your selected profession. This article will manual you through key factors of expert development, which incorporates setting dreams, searching out mentorship, increasing your skillset, and preserving a piece-life stability. By that specialize within the ones regions, you can continuously make bigger and excel in your full-time position.

Setting Professional Development Goals:

Setting easy and measurable professional improvement goals is vital for charting your increase and development. Here's how you could set powerful desires:

Identify Areas for Growth: Reflect for your strengths and weaknesses, and recognize regions in which you want to enhance or collect new skills. Consider each technical abilities unique in your field and smooth abilities, at the facet of management, communication, or time manipulate.

Align Goals with Organizational Objectives: Understand the desires and goals of your organisation or department. Align your professional development dreams with the ones desires to ensure that your boom contributes to the general fulfillment of the enterprise.

Make Goals SMART: Ensure that your desires are Specific, Measurable, Achievable, Relevant, and Time-tremendous (SMART). For example, in place of setting a indistinct motive like "beautify communication talents," make it precise thru declaring, "participate in a public speaking workshop and deliver 3 shows inner six months."

Break Goals into Milestones: Break down your extended-time period dreams into smaller milestones or quick-term desires. This technique permits you to tune improvement and have a very good time achievements along the manner.

Regularly Review and Adjust Goals: Regularly evaluation and look into your desires to make sure they remain relevant and aligned collectively along with your career trajectory. Adjust them as wanted based totally on new possibilities or changes in your professional aspirations.

Seeking Mentorship and Guidance:

Mentorship performs a vital position in professional development, offering steering, assist, and treasured insights from professional specialists to your concern.

Here's how you can are looking for mentorship:

Identify Potential Mentors: Identify human beings inside your organisation or agency who non-public the abilities, information, and enjoy you recognize. Look for experts who are approachable, supportive, and willing to put money into your growth.

Reach Out and Establish Connections: Approach potential mentors and express your hobby in their steerage. Request a meeting or a verbal exchange to talk approximately your career goals and are attempting to find their recommendation. Personalize your request and deliver an motive for why you don't forget they might be a treasured mentor.

Be Prepared and Respectful: When meeting with a capability mentor, come organized with unique questions or topics you would like to talk about. Respect their time and display authentic interest in their insights and studies.

Maintain Regular Communication: Establish a regular cadence of communique together along with your mentor. This can be through scheduled conferences, emails, or cellular telephone calls. Update them in your progress, are searching for advice on challenges, and proportion successes.

Act on Feedback: Be open to comments and guidelines supplied through manner of your mentor. Actively work on implementing their recommendation and tips to beautify your professional increase. Regularly talk your improvement and are trying to find similarly steering as wanted.

Pay it Forward: As you development to your career, preserve in mind turning into a mentor to others. Share your records and testimonies to assist the development of destiny experts in your concern.

Expanding Your Skillset:

Continuous getting to know and potential improvement are critical for staying relevant and advancing for your profession. Here are strategies to extend your skillset:

Attend Workshops, Conferences, and Webinars: Participate in industry-related workshops, meetings, and webinars. These events provide opportunities to analyze from professionals, advantage insights into developing tendencies, and network with specialists for your area.

Pursue Professional Certifications: Identify applicable professional certifications or credentials in your organization. These certifications showcase your strength of mind to non-prevent mastering and might decorate your credibility and marketability.

Seek Cross-Functional Experiences: Look for opportunities to artwork on move-sensible obligations or collaborate with colleagues from special departments. This exposure broadens your skillset and information of approaches unique elements of the agency function.

Embrace Online Learning: Take benefit of on line studying systems that offer a massive shape of publications and tutorials. Platforms like LinkedIn Learning, Coursera, and Udemy offer flexibility in selecting guides that align together with your pastimes and profession desires.

Seek Stretch Assignments: Volunteer for difficult assignments or responsibilities that push you out of your comfort area. These possibilities will will let you expand new talents, display off your abilities, and display your readiness for advanced responsibilities.

Foster a Learning Culture: Cultivate a gaining knowledge of mind-set inside your group or business enterprise. Share information, encourage collaboration, and create possibilities for non-prevent getting to know and potential-sharing amongst colleagues.

Maintaining Work-Life Balance:

Achieving a healthy paintings-life stability is vital for popular nicely-being and sustained achievement in your career. Here are a few techniques to help you preserve this balance:

Set Boundaries: Establish easy obstacles between artwork and personal existence. Define particular times forwork-related sports sports and prioritize private time for relaxation, hobbies, and spending time with cherished ones.

Practice Effective Time Management: Learn to govern some time effectively through prioritizing responsibilities, delegating even as essential, and fending off procrastination. Use productiveness strategies together with the Pomodoro Technique or time-blocking off to maximise your attention and productivity.

Take Regular Breaks: Avoid burnout with the resource of taking ordinary breaks at some point of the workday. Engage in sports that assist you recharge, which includes going for a walk, operating in the course of mindfulness, or venture a hobby.

Communicate and Negotiate: Openly communicate along facet your supervisors and buddies approximately your art work-existence stability dreams. Negotiate flexible paintings preparations if feasible, which incorporates far off artwork, flexible hours, or compressed workweeks.

Practice Self-Care: Prioritize self-care sports, together with exercising, proper vitamins, and sufficient sleep. Taking care of your physical and highbrow nicely-being is vital for retaining a healthy paintings-lifestyles stability.

Disconnect from Work: Establish barriers with generation thru disconnecting from paintings-associated emails and notifications out of doors of running hours. Create particular "unplugged" periods to attention on personal sports sports and rest.

Cultivate Supportive Relationships: Surround yourself with a supportive network of buddies, circle of relatives, and co-employees who understand the importance of labor-life balance. Lean on them for assist, recommendation, and encouragement.

Regularly Assess and Adjust: Regularly observe your paintings-life stability and make changes as wanted. Priorities also can shift through the years, so be bendy and willing to conform your technique to hold a healthy equilibrium.

BALANCING WORK AND EDUCATION

In a quick-paced and traumatic worldwide, private productivity is critical for undertaking success and keeping a healthy work-life stability. This article explores techniques and techniques to decorate personal productiveness, together with time control, intention setting, prioritization, and stress manage. By implementing the ones strategies, people can optimize their basic performance, boom overall performance, and attain their favored outcomes.

Time Management:

Effective time manage is the cornerstone of private productiveness. Here are a few strategies that will help you make the maximum of some time:

Prioritize Tasks: Start by means of the use of identifying and prioritizing responsibilities based totally on their significance and urgency. Use techniques like Eisenhower's Urgent-Important Matrix to categorize obligations and attention on immoderate-priority sports.

Set Clear Goals: Establish clear and specific desires to guide your actions. Break massive desires into smaller, functionality duties to cause them to extra possible and lots much less overwhelming.

Create a Schedule: Develop a every day or weekly agenda that allocates time for each mission and hobby. Use equipment like calendars, planners, or digital productiveness apps to help you live prepared and heading within the proper path.

Avoid Procrastination: Procrastination can forestall productivity. Combat it thru breaking duties into smaller, practicable chunks, placing remaining dates, and the usage of strategies much like the Pomodoro Technique (walking in targeted intervals with short breaks) to keep momentum.

Delegate and Outsource: Learn to delegate responsibilities that can be treated thru way of others. Identify areas wherein you may outsource or are attempting to find help, releasing up some time to attention on high-price activities.

Eliminate Time Wasters: Identify and do away with sports activities or behavior that consume time without contributing in your productivity. Minimize distractions, along with excessive social media use, and create a conducive art work surroundings.

Continuous Learning and Improvement: Invest time in getting to know and improving your abilities. This ongoing improvement permits you to work greater effectively and live earlier in your problem.

Goal Setting

Setting clean and massive dreams is instrumental in the use of non-public productivity. Here are techniques for effective intention setting:

SMART Goals: Use the SMART framework (Specific, Measurable, Achievable, Relevant, Time-wonderful) to set dreams which may be nicely-described, practical, and time-high quality. This framework allows you create desires which might be actionable and aligned together together with your common goals.

Break Goals Down: Break big desires into smaller, capability milestones. This approach presents a experience of improvement and allows for a step-by using way of-step technique, growing motivation and momentum.

Visualize Success: Visualize yourself reaching your dreams and the superb outcomes associated with them. This method allows preserve popularity, motivation, and a exceptional mind-set.

Review and Adjust: Regularly evaluation your dreams and take a look at your development. Make important adjustments or realignments based totally totally on changing instances or new insights. Flexibility is high to making sure your desires stay relevant and doable.

Accountability and Tracking: Hold yourself answerable for your goals. Track your development, have amusing milestones, and pick out out regions for development. Consider sharing your desires with a depended on buddy, mentor, or obligation companion who can offer help and assist preserve you heading within the proper direction.

Reward System: Establish a praise gadget for accomplishing your desires. Celebrate your accomplishments and deal with yourself for attaining milestones. This great reinforcement complements motivation and will increase pleasure.

Prioritization:

Prioritization is crucial for personal productiveness, allowing you to cognizance on immoderate-price responsibilities and make efficient use of it slow. Here are techniques for powerful prioritization:

Urgency and Importance: Assess the urgency and importance of responsibilities to decide their precedence. Focus on responsibilities which have coming close to deadlines or super effect on your desires.

ABC Method: Use the ABC method to categorize responsibilities as A (excessive priority), B (medium priority), or C (low priority). This method permits you allocate it sluggish and property correctly.

Consider Impact: Consider the ability impact of each venture on your regular productiveness and favored outcomes. Prioritize duties which have a large have an effect on for your desires or that make a contribution to extended-term fulfillment.

Time vs. Value: Evaluate obligations primarily based completely totally on the time required to finish them and the price they create about. Prioritize obligations that offer the most price relative to the time invested.

Focus on One Task at a Time: Multitasking can reduce overall performance and bring about mistakes. Instead, reputation on one challenge at a time, giving it your whole hobby in advance than transferring without delay to the following.

Learn to Say No: Recognize your limitations and look at to mention no to obligations or commitments that do not align together with your priorities or stretch your private home too skinny. This lets in you to protect it gradual and dedicate it to sports activities that virtually rely.

Stress Management:

Effective stress manipulate is vital for keeping non-public productivity and standard well-being. Here are strategies to help you control and decrease strain:

Identify Stressors: Identify the belongings of pressure on your existence, each at art work and in your non-public lifestyles. Awareness of these stressors permits you to amplify targeted techniques to mitigate their impact and assemble resilience.

Time for Self-Care: Prioritize self-care activities that sell relaxation, rejuvenation, and ordinary properly-being. Engage in sports activities activities including exercising, meditation, pastimes, and spending time with cherished ones to recharge and reduce strain.

Healthy Work-Life Balance: Establish barriers among art work and personal lifestyles. Set aside devoted time for rest, enjoyment sports sports, and spending time with family and pals. Avoid overworking or bringing paintings-associated pressure into your private lifestyles.

Effective Communication: Improve conversation talents to reduce misunderstandings and conflicts that may contribute to pressure. Clearly explicit your wishes, issues, and obstacles, each at paintings and in personal relationships.

Time for Reflection: Incorporate normal pondered photograph and self-assessment into your ordinary. Evaluate your strain ranges, emerge as aware of triggers, and find out strategies to higher control stressors. This self-cognizance lets in for proactive strain control.

Breaks and Rest: Incorporate normal breaks into your workday to recharge and save you burnout. Short breaks at some point of the day can help preserve consciousness and productivity. Additionally, make certain you get sufficient sleep to assist physical and highbrow properly-being.

Support Network: Cultivate a manual community of buddies, circle of relatives, or colleagues who can offer emotional help and steering. Seek assist at the identical time as preferred and do not hesitate to acquire out to experts if pressure turns into overwhelming.

Time Management Techniques: Implement effective time manipulate strategies, as noted in advance, to reduce strain because of feeling overwhelmed or rushed.

Stress Reduction Techniques: Explore stress discount techniques which include deep respiratory physical activities, mindfulness, yoga, or journaling. These practices can assist calm the thoughts, lessen tension, and enhance commonplace nicely-being.

REFLECTING ON YOUR APPRENTICESHIP EXPERIENCE

The very last contact of an apprenticeship marks a splendid milestone in one's career adventure. Taking the time to reflect on the revel in lets in apprentices to advantage valuable insights which can form their future paths. Here are some key components to maintain in thoughts at a few degree within the reflected picture way:

Accomplishments: Reflect on the achievements and milestones attained for the duration of your apprenticeship. Consider the talents you have got were given obtained, duties you've got were given finished, and any recognition or first-rate feedback acquired. Celebrate your accomplishments and widely diagnosed the development made.

Challenges and Lessons Learned: Reflect on the challenges encountered in some unspecified time in the future of your apprenticeship. Identify the instructions observed from the ones evaluations, in conjunction with problem-fixing abilties, resilience, adaptability, and the capability to work below stress. Recognize the boom that has took place because of overcoming those challenges.

Mentorship and Guidance: Evaluate the help and steering received from mentors, supervisors, and co-human beings sooner or later of your apprenticeship. Consider the effect that they had for your studying and professional improvement. Reflect on the relationships constructed and the understanding obtained from those interactions.

Personal Growth: Reflect on how the apprenticeship enjoy has contributed in your non-public boom. Assess the development of your paintings ethic, time control talents, energy of will, and capability to art work independently. Consider any improvements in yourself assurance, communique capabilities, and trouble-fixing abilities.

Work Environment and Company Culture: Evaluate the art work surroundings and agency life-style in that you completed your apprenticeship. Consider how the ones factors precipitated your revel in and expert boom. Reflect on whether or no longer the values and dreams of the organization align together with your private aspirations.

Chapter 11: Understanding Yourself

Welcome, extra younger trailblazers, to the coronary heart of your adventure - the exhilarating exploration of self. In this monetary break, we embark on a voyage of self-discovery, delving deep into the treasure trove of your being to unearth the jewels that outline your essence.

Values and Personality Assessment:

Imagine your values because of the truth the guiding stars that slight up the path of your lifestyles' journey. By identifying those guiding lights, you advantage clarity approximately what in truth subjects to you, shaping your alternatives and actions in alignment along with your internal maximum convictions. Take a 2nd to mirror on what brings you pleasure, what stirs your soul, and what ignites the fireplace internal. These are the clues that lead you for your passions and interests, lights the way toward a profession that resonates with your coronary heart.

Next, permit us to flip our gaze inward to discover the kaleidoscope of your individual. You are a masterpiece, crafted with unique hues and sun sun shades that paint the canvas of your man or woman. Through introspection and self-attention, you solve the problematic tapestry of your personality, identifying your strengths, quirks, and idiosyncrasies. Welcome the quirks that make you, you, for therein lies your finest electricity. Celebrate your strengths and welcome your weaknesses, for they're the building blocks of your increase and improvement.

Skills and Aptitudes:

Within the garden of your being lie seeds of capability prepared to blossom. Take a moment to survey this landscape, for inside it lays the key to unlocking your actual capability. Recognize your natural abilities and areas for development; for they may be the device with that you sculpt your future. Whether you very own the present of creativity, the prowess of analytical questioning, or the finesse of conversation, each skill is a valuable gem geared up to be polished.

But do not be disheartened through the usage of regions of increase, for they may be the fertile soil wherein your potential prospers. Welcome demanding conditions as possibilities for growth, for it is thru perseverance and backbone that you cultivate mastery. Remember, the journey of self-improvement is not a sprint but a marathon, with each breakthrough bringing you in the direction of the summit of your aspirations.

Learning Styles and Preferences:

Just as every flower blooms in its very very very own time and way, so too does anybody thrive in special getting to know environments. Take a 2nd to reflect on the way you outstanding take in and gadget data. Are you a seen learner, who flourishes on diagrams and illustrations? Or possibly you are an auditory learner, who learns first-class thru lectures and discussions. Maybe you are a kinesthetic learner, who learns through arms-on experience and experimentation. Whatever your studying fashion, welcome it wholeheartedly, for it is the critical factor that unlocks the door on your whole capacity.

But do now not limit your self to at the least one mode of analyzing, for the area is a rich tapestry of research geared up to be explored. Experiment with precise studying strategies, for it is through variety which you beautify your information and develop your horizons. Welcome the delight of lifelong mastering, for it is thru interest and exploration which you unleash the boundless capability inside.

As you embark in this journey of self-discovery, undergo in mind which you are the architect of your future. Welcome the adventure with open hands and an adventurous spirit, for interior you lies the electricity to form your desires into reality. With every leap ahead, may additionally you discover new sides of your being and emerge stronger, wiser, and additional empowered than ever in advance than.

Exploring Career Options

Welcome, younger adventurers, to the gateway of limitless opportunities - the arena of profession exploration. In this bankruptcy, we embark on a exciting tour via the large landscape of possibilities, guided with the aid of the compass of interest and fueled with the resource of the winds of ambition.

Researching Different Industries and Occupations:

Picture yourself as an intrepid explorer, starting off to map the uncharted territories of the professional worldwide. Armed with the gear of modern-day-day technology, you delve into the labyrinth of on-line assets, profession courses, and informational interviews. These assets are your treasure map, guiding you toward hidden gems of notion and understanding.

Start by manner of the use of casting your internet huge, exploring a severa array of industries and occupations. From healthcare to technology, from education to finance, the possibilities are as good sized due to the fact the celebrities inside the night time time sky. Immerse your self in the rich tapestry of each organization, gaining insights into its particular manner of life, tendencies, and possibilities. Pay interest to the recollections of those who have trodden the course earlier than you, for his or her critiques offer useful commands and concept.

As you navigate this virtual landscape, allow your interest be your compass. Dive deep into the intricacies of every business organisation, asking probing questions and seeking out mentors who can shed mild at the course ahead. Remember, expertise is energy, and the greater approximately the arena of work, the higher organized you'll be to make informed decisions about your destiny.

Shadowing Professionals and Volunteering:

But exploration isn't restricted to the location of our on-line world; every now and then, the most treasured insights are acquired through firsthand enjoy. Imagine yourself as a silent observer, shadowing specialists of their herbal habitat. Whether it's far a bustling sanatorium ward, a bustling tech startup, or a serene nature reserve, every art work surroundings gives a unique window into the arena of work.

Reach out to experts in your preferred challenge, expressing your eagerness to investigate and grow. Offer to volunteer it slow and strength in trade for the possibility to shadow them and advantage firsthand enjoy. Observe their each day workout routines, ask questions, and take within the consciousness they impart. Remember, every interplay is an opportunity to have a take a look at and increase, so technique every experience with an open thoughts and a spirit of hobby.

Volunteering is every different valuable street for exploration, presenting you the possibility to make a difference while gaining precious insights into capacity career paths. Whether it is volunteering at a community clinic, a community center, or an environmental business enterprise, every revel in broadens your horizons and deepens your know-how of the world spherical you. Welcome the ones opportunities with enthusiasm and self-control, for they will be the stepping stones that lead you inside the path of your goals.

Assessing Job Outlook and Salary Potential:

As you task deeper into the place of career exploration, it's miles important to hold one eye at the horizon of practicality. Consider the task outlook and profits capability of diverse career paths, weighing the opportunities towards your personal aspirations and values. While passion fuels your dreams, practicality ensures their sustainability ultimately.

Chapter 12: Smart Goals For Success

Welcome, bold young dreamers, to the gateway of achievement - the place of SMART goals. In this economic damage, we embark on a adventure of empowerment and transformation, harnessing the energy of readability and intention to show desires into truth.

Setting Specific Goals:

Imagine your desires because of the fact the stars that guide your journey thru the night sky. Specificity is the telescope thru which you attention your gaze, honing in at the objectives that slight up the darkness. Be smooth and specific approximately what you want to attain, defining your dreams with clarity and specificity. Instead of aiming to "get better at math," try to "decorate my algebra abilties via finishing three exercise troubles every day." The extra precise your desires, the clearer your course becomes.

Setting Measurable Goals:

Measurability is the compass that tracks your progress alongside the path of success. Just as a traveler marks every milestone on their journey, so too need to you diploma your improvement towards your dreams. Break down your dreams into tangible metrics and milestones, permitting you to music your development and characteristic fun your achievements alongside the manner. Instead of aiming to "study greater books," set a intention to "look at 20 pages every day," allowing you to degree your improvement and modify your direction as wanted.

Setting Achievable Goals:

Achievability is the fuel that powers your journey toward fulfillment. While it is important to dream huge, it's far similarly important to set goals which can be inner your gain. Be realistic approximately your abilities and sources, setting desires that reach your limits with out breaking them. Instead of aiming to "become a international-renowned artist in a single day," set a aim to "entire a painting workshop and display off my artwork at a neighborhood gallery." By setting manageable goals, you region your self up for success and assemble momentum towards your dreams.

Setting Relevant Goals:

Relevance is the North Star that guides your journey within the route of fulfillment. Just as a sailor aligns their path with the prevailing winds, so too want to you align your dreams together collectively together with your values, passions, and aspirations. Ensure that your desires are applicable for your lengthy-time period vision and contribute in your today's increase and happiness. Instead of chasing after desires that society dictates, pursue those who resonate together with your coronary coronary heart and soul. By setting relevant desires, you infuse your journey with motive and meaning.

Setting Time-certain Goals:

Time is the forex of fulfillment, and setting last dates is the key to unlocking its energy. Just as a vacationer devices a reduce-off date for achieving their vacation spot, so too must you positioned closing dates for attaining your dreams. Be unique about at the same time as you need to gather each milestone, developing a revel in of urgency and reputation that propels you in advance. Instead of leaving your goals open-ended, set a last date for every milestone, allowing you to music your development and live accountable.

As you embark on the adventure of placing SMART desires, bear in mind that you are the architect of your future. With clarity of vision and purpose, you have got the strength to show your desires into truth. Welcome the method with enthusiasm and determination, for every bounce ahead brings you within the route of the life you envision. With SMART goals as your guiding moderate, may moreover you navigate the seas of achievement with self belief and purpose.

Short-Term and Long-Term Goals

Welcome, younger visionaries, to the crossroads of opportunity - the intersection of short-time period and lengthy-time period dreams. In this bankruptcy, we embark on a journey of strategic planning and visionary questioning, crafting a roadmap that bridges the triumphing with the future.

Planning for Immediate Steps:

Imagine your short-term desires as stepping stones that lead you across the river of opportunity. These dreams are the right away actions you're taking to propel your self forward closer to your long-term vision. They provide you with path and momentum, guiding you towards your final destination.

Start with the resource of identifying the quick-time period dreams a good way to circulate you inside the course of your desires. These might be small, actionable steps that you could take in recent times, the following day, or in the following few months.

Whether it's miles completing a certification route, gaining experience thru internships, or networking with specialists in your area, each quick-time period cause brings you one step inside the route of your lengthy-term aspirations.

Planning for Future Aspirations:

But while quick-time period desires are the stepping stones that manual your at once adventure, prolonged-time period desires are the North Star that publications your overarching imaginative and prescient. These dreams are the dreams and aspirations that define your future, presenting you with a experience of cause and course.

Chapter 13: Creating An Action Plan

Welcome, architects of your destiny, to the blueprint of success - the place of movement making plans. In this bankruptcy, we roll up our sleeves and dive into the nitty-gritty of goal implementation, breaking down desires into actionable steps and remodeling imaginative and prescient into truth.

Breaking Down Goals into Manageable Steps:

Imagine your desires as a mountain prepared to be conquered. While the summit may additionally additionally seem daunting from afar, breaking it down into doable steps makes the ascent greater doable. Start via dissecting your goals into smaller, chew-sized duties that you may address one at a time.

Take your prolonged-time period goals and spoil them down into quarterly, monthly, and weekly milestones. Each milestone turns into a checkpoint on your adventure, guiding your improvement and keeping you on path. By breaking your desires down into workable steps, you create a roadmap that transforms daunting desires into practicable realities.

Setting Deadlines:

Time is the foreign exchange of achievement, and remaining dates are the milestones that mark your progress along the adventure. Just as vacationer units a last date for accomplishing their holiday spot, so too need to you put remaining dates for task your desires. Be precise about at the identical time as you need to complete every challenge, developing a revel in of urgency and popularity that propels you beforehand.

But keep in mind, closing dates are not set in stone; they're flexible publications that adapt to the twists and turns of your journey. Be practical approximately your timeframes and regulate them as had to accommodate surprising traumatic situations and possibilities. By putting closing dates, you create a enjoy of obligation that drives you inside the route of fulfillment.

Identifying Resources:

No journey is taken on my own, and no reason is completed in isolation. Identify the belongings you need to manual your adventure, whether or not it is financial, instructional, or emotional assist. Reach out to mentors, pals, and experts to your region for steerage and advice. Invest in system and belongings as a way to beneficial useful resource your boom and development, whether or not or now not it is books, guides, or era.

But consider, the maximum valuable useful resource you very own is your own resilience and determination. Cultivate a mindset of perseverance and adaptableness, for it is through resilience that you conquer stressful situations and emerge stronger than in advance than. With the proper sources and thoughts-set, there's no reason too massive, no dream too formidable to build up.

As you embark on the journey of movement planning, take into account which you hold the pen that writes the story of your lifestyles. With willpower in your coronary coronary heart and a clean imaginative and prescient in your mind, you've got the strength to show goals into fact. Welcome the approach with enthusiasm and perseverance, for each leap beforehand brings you in the path of the existence you envision. With movement making plans as your guiding compass, also can you navigate the seas of fulfillment with self perception and reason?

Overcoming Obstacles and Staying Motivated

Welcome, resilient souls, to the crucible of project and triumph - the area wherein goals meet adversity, and perseverance reigns ideally suited. In this financial ruin, we embark on a journey of resilience and resolution, equipping ourselves with the device to overcome obstacles and live inspired on the route to achievement.

Recognizing Challenges:

Life is a tapestry woven with threads of satisfaction and sorrow, triumph and tribulation. Along your journey of career planning and purpose placing, you will truly stumble upon boundaries that check your remedy and venture your willpower. These limitations can also take many office work - from self-doubt and worry of failure to outside challenges which include monetary constraints or societal expectations.

The first step in overcoming limitations is to understand them for what they may be - brief roadblocks on the route for your desires. Instead of viewing annoying situations as insurmountable obstacles, see them as possibilities for growth and studying. Welcome every impediment as a stepping stone within the direction of your fulfillment, for it is through overcoming adversity which you forge the energy and resilience to gain your desires.

www.ingramcontent.com/pod-product-compliance
Lightning Source LLC
Chambersburg PA
CBHW070555010526
44118CB00012B/1321